Seeds *and* propagation

SMITH & HAWKEN

The Hands·On Gardener

Seeds *and* propagation

by SUSAN MCCLURE

with illustrations

by JIM ANDERSON

WORKMAN PUBLISHING · NEW YORK

ACKNOWLEGDMENTS

Seeds and propagation, both subjects I keenly enjoy, were a pleasure to write about thanks to friends and associates who helped along the way. I applaud Judy Batdorff and Robin Siktberg, researchers and garden designers in Cleveland for valuable information shared; Dave Schultz, formerly of Springbrook Gardens perennial nursery for his assistance with root cuttings; Joyce Dyer of Hiram College for her advice on voice, an intriguing element of writing; and Denise Yankee, Propagation Supervisor of Lake County Nursery Exchange for her assistance with hardwood cuttings. I'd also like to mention my wonderful garden in Cleveland, Ohio, a great place to experiment with propagation techniques, now sadly left behind with a move to the Chicago area.

Library of Congress Cataloging-in-Publication Data
McClure, Susan, 1957–
Seeds and propagation / by Susan McClure; illustrations by Jim Anderson
p. cm.—(Smith & Hawken—the hands-on gardener)
Includes index.
ISBN 0-7611-0733-9
1. Plant propagation. 2. Seeds I. Anderson, Jim. II. Title
III. Series.
SB119.M33 1997
635' .043—dc21   97-5745
CIP

Workman Publishing Company
708 Broadway, New York, NY 10003-9555

Manufactured in the United States of America

First printing April 1997

10 9 8 7 6 5 4 3 2 1

CONTENTS

A SEEDS *and* PROPAGATION PRIMER

S imple pleasures are scarce today, which makes them even more rare and valuable. Yet they abound in the garden where the most tranquil tasks—sowing seeds, taking cuttings, making divisions—can bring to life a surprising number of plants. With these new plants come the pleasure of nurturing and the joy of watching a tiny sprout grow, flower, and fruit. That a magnificent oak or a perfumed flower will rise from one tiny seed, encouraged by our loving efforts, is a miracle that enriches us.

Our ancestors had to create life—growing their own foods, fibers, and medicines—to sustain themselves and were much closer to the cycles of nature than most of us are today. They had an intimate link to the garden; they were dependent on it, fortified by it, and totally in awe of its power. This gave their lives fullness and purpose, as eloquently described by Thomas Jefferson when he said, "No occupation is so delightful to me as the culture of the earth and no culture comparable to that of the garden." The garden remains a place to stay intimately in touch with the earth's cycles of birth, death, and rebirth.

Propagating, sowing, dividing—returning to garden basics—brings us a similar delight and peace. Although it is no longer necessary for our survival, propagation adds a special dimension to our lives. It is surprisingly easy to harness the tremendous power of working hand-in-hand with nature, and anyone can do it. Enjoying the vigor of a plant started from a root cutting or the exotic beauty of a rare flower available only to those who plant a seed is well worth the effort. Planting our roots in the garden and bringing life from the soil are elemental acts that give great contentment.

There are many practical advantages to propagation. It is an inexpensive way to fill our gardens with diverse, high-quality plant life. A choice shrub can be multiplied into many by taking cuttings, or a favorite flower can sprout by the dozens from a two dollar packet of seeds. Gardeners who propagate have a wider variety of plants and vegetables available to them other than just those that are commercially propagated and sold in nurseries. Some cannot be obtained in any way other than by propagation. Growing these young upstarts simply with clean water and natural organic products keeps our gardens pure and the environment clean.

Propagation seems almost like magic. But starting with one plant or one packet of seed and turning it into several involves no sleight of hand, just basic botany.

The awe-inspiring regenerative powers of plants are the basis of all types of propagation. The blueprint for an entire plant hides within a seed, bud, or bulb, allowing plants to arise from the tiny resting structures we call seeds or to regenerate missing pieces. All the gardener needs to do is provide judicious timing and some simple soils and tools.

Seeds, which need nurturing early on, can provide dozens of young plants. If seedlings are started from carefully bred hybrids, they will grow into startlingly similar plants. If they are grown from open-pollinated seeds, which allow nature to shuffle the parents' genetic deck, the offspring can grow into a range of different plants, which are a delight for an informal garden. Quick-growing annuals such as basil and zinnias, which finish their garden performance within a single garden year, are a snap to sow directly into the garden soil. Other plants, such as slow-starting perennials, shrubs, or trees, can take much longer and require extra supervision to reach self-sustaining maturity.

Among the most remarkable performers are the plants that arise from stem and root cuttings. Given a healthy section of firm young stem, a slender woody branch, or a strapping young root, many plants can sprout the parts that are missing and become whole again. Fast-growing annuals such as coleus are especially adept at growing from stem cuttings. A piece of shoot stuck in a glass of water quickly gives rise to roots. Tip cuttings of chrysanthemums and dahlias, set in peat-based potting mix, root equally fast and can finish the first growing season looking as lush and beautiful as their parent plant. Although they move a little slower, stem cuttings of some shrubs such as lilacs and viburnums will become self-sufficient much more quickly than their seedlings. Root cuttings are easy to borrow from a thriving perennial flower or herb with spreading roots or rhizomes. The mother plant quickly regenerates her lost roots and the root cuttings yield a bonanza of new plants.

Perennial flowers, which spread outward in waves of lush new growth, are particularly suited to division, a form of propagation in which sections of plants are severed, rooted, and grown to maturity. A parent plant is unearthed and sectioned into pieces having as little as a single root and shoot bud, each of which will grow into a new plant. Plants with young limbs that cascade toward the ground can produce a new plant from a single buried stem. A small but deliberate injury to a rhododendron stem and a soft blanket of moist soil and mulch are the genesis of a strapping new start.

There is nothing comparable to the thrill of creating new life on your windowsills, or seeing flowers growing in the garden that you've started on the kitchen table. With the simplest of tools, a minimum of supplies, and a little bit of knowledge, you can participate in this miracle of regeneration.

PROPAGATION EQUIPMENT

Propagation comes close to getting something for nothing, but it does require the purchase of some basic supplies. These can be obtained readily and at minimal expense. More sophisticated equipment, designed to give amateur gardeners professional results, is also available, but is not essential to successful home propagation. Avid propagators, however, may want to invest in high-tech propagating equipment.

Buying high-quality goods that will last for years rather than products designed for one-time use is strongly recommended. Although good quality supplies will cost a little more initially, in the long run, they are more economical and environmentally responsible than disposable products.

For example, white plastic labels, available for five to ten cents each, may last only weeks or months before they break or are pushed out of the soil and lost. A few new tags a year might be necessary to mark just one plant. However, aluminum plant labels, rectangular tags atop 10"-long legs, can cost seventy-five cents each. Because they do not rust, break, or get lost in the garden soil, they can be on the job for twenty years or so.

Thrifty propagators can recycle ordinary household leftovers into propagating containers and accessories. Common yogurt cups, washed and sterilized, make fine seedling containers. Recycled plastic spoons, written on with permanent ink markers, can make temporary labels for plants.

Many propagating supplies are available locally at garden centers or in department store garden areas. Basic containers, peat-based planting mixes, and labels are standard items that are widely distributed. Full-service garden centers, agricultural supply houses, and mail-order specialists will stock more specialized propagating equipment such as heating cables or soil blockers or will order them for you at the ordinary retail price.

Basic and specialty items are also available from mail-order catalogs, which are the ultimate in convenience and selection. Seed, garden supply, and nursery catalogs generally offer a wide range of propagation supplies.

Containers

Containers hold planting mix or soil and help form an environment suitable for root growth of plants, cuttings, seedlings, and small divisions or layered stems. The choice of container determines the amount of space and level of vital elements, such as oxygen and moisture. As when freezing bumper harvests of beans in freezer containers or canning them in approved canning jars, you should select a container that is best suited for the type of propagation you are undertaking. The size of the plant part you are propagating, the amount of moisture it needs, and the length of time it will remain in the original container all influence this choice.

Begin with containers that have holes in the bottom to allow excess moisture to drain out. Many decorative pots have solid bottoms—without provisions for drainage—and are not appropriate for propagation. Pots that are suitable can vary, their size altering the growing conditions inside.

Small containers 1"–2" in diameter can be ideal for growing a single seedling or cutting, keeping its roots separate from any other plants you may have propagated at the same time. But small containers dry out and heat up more quickly than large pots.

For roomier accommodations, seedlings or cuttings can be started

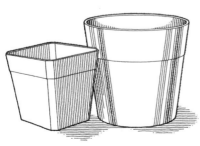

Plastic pots are easily stacked for storage.

in pots that are 3"–4" in diameter. If space is limited, look for square pots that fit together snugly on a windowsill or in a light garden.

Another option is to plant several seeds or cuttings in 6" or 8" pots, which hold more moisture and provide more rooting room than smaller pots. In a 6" pot, for example, four lettuce seedlings can start nicely. Two large tomato seedlings might grow side by side in an 8" pot until ready to set out in the garden. If you grow several plants in one large container, the plants will have to be separated and transplanted into individual pots or the garden before they become entangled in one another. Repotting requires an investment in time but the results are well worth the effort.

PLASTIC CONTAINERS: Versatile plastics of many types are molded into a variety of different shaped containers that all share some common characteristics. Plastic forms a dense barrier that limits oxygen exchange except through the pot's top opening and bottom drainage holes. Limited oxygen exchange can be a benefit, slowing the rate soils dry out in hot weather, but it will not help an excessively wet soil dry out in cool weather. Plastics are lightweight, easy to transport, and great for balcony gardens. But they are not as stable as clay pots and are liable to tip over in a windy environment or when filled with tall or top-heavy plants.

The rigid sheet-type plastics commonly used for pots and flats are available in subtle greens and blacks as well as bolder colors for designer looks. Although more accident-proof than breakable clay or ceramic pots, these plastics are likely to crack and break if exposed to extensive sun and winter cold. This is especially true of lightweight plastics intended for one-time use. Alternatively, some propagating containers are made of strong, flexible, resilient plastic foams that can last for years if handled carefully. Environmentally conscious gardeners may prefer containers made of recycled plastics, which also are available.

Plastic pots come in round or square shapes and sizes varying from 1" to 50" or more in diameter. Propagators tend to use 3"-, 4"-, 6"-, or even 8"-diameter pots; professional nurserymen also use quart pots and 1- and 2-gallon pots for larger perennials and shrubs. Compared with flats, cell packs, and plug trays (descriptions follow), pots take up extra room when seedlings are small but some can support young plants (and

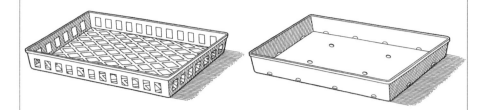

Netted flats are good for holding homemade pots such as yogurt cups. Solid flats with drainage holes work well without any pots at all.

young stem cuttings) from the time they are started until they are ready to go outside.

Plastics are used to make flats—long, shallow, rectangular propagating containers that usually measure 11" × 22" or 10" × 20" and are about 2½" deep. Flats work best for starting a large number of plants in rows or staggered square plantings.

Flats can be netted or solid, with or without drainage holes. Each has a different purpose; netted flats will hold cell packs or pots, but have too many openings to hold planting mix. Solid flats with drainage holes in the bottom can be planted with seedlings or cuttings or used to house individual containers. Either kind of flat can be slipped into watering trays—solid plastic flats without drainage holes—that are filled with water or a dilute fertilizer solution. This process is called bottom watering and allows individual containers to absorb needed moisture. The propagating flat should be removed from the watering tray after several minutes to prevent oversaturating the soil.

If sowing or planting directly in a flat, gardeners should plan to transplant seedlings or cuttings while moderately small into containers that allow each one more growing room. To make this process easier, experienced gardeners will plant community flats with species that develop at similar rates. Then they can all be transplanted at the same time, simply and effectively.

Cell packs are plastic packs of four, six, eight, or more cells, each cell providing enough room for a single seedling to get a solid start.

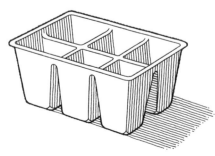

Cell packs with larger openings can hold seedlings longer than other containers.

Once seedlings have used up all the available rooting space, they can be transplanted directly into the garden or put into larger pots. Cell packs are more convenient than planting in an undivided community flat but require careful watering. Cells that are missed with the watering can even one time may dry out, killing the seedling inside. If allowed to linger too long in a cell pack, they may become rootbound, a condition in which a plant's roots wind around the perimeter of the pot creating a solid mat of tissue. Roots in this condition cannot grow out into the soil and are ineffective.

Cell packs used for greenhouse-grown bedding annuals or vegetable seedlings are generally made of lightweight plastics that can be sterilized (see page 16) and reused. The thin plastic makes removing seedlings easy. You can squeeze or push up through the thin plastic cell to pop out the rootball without damaging the roots. If you buy a better grade of plastic that is not as easily maneuvered, you will have to pull the seedling out carefully from the top. For easy off-season storage, identical size cell packs can be nested together.

Plug trays have individual planting cells for seedlings, but the cells can be much smaller than those in cell packs and are combined into a flat-sized tray. Originally developed for mechanized nursery seed plant-

HOW TO BUILD A HOMEMADE FLAT

Wooden flats can be constructed easily at home, assuming you have the work space. The best material is untreated pine or fir. Nail together a frame from 4"-wide shelving lumber, small enough to be moved easily when filled with planting mix. (Nursery flats are about 13"×20"; galvanized 1½" finishing nails are recommended.)

Turn the four-sided frame over, and nail slats across the bottom, using shelving lumber. To provide for drainage, leave a ¼" space between each piece. Cut wire coat hangers (with slip pliers or wire cutters) and bend them into hoops that extend across the width of the flat. Fill the flat with planting mix to a depth of 2" to 3", and insert hoops to form a covered wagon. When the flat is inserted into a plastic bag, secure with a twist tie to keep moisture in.

ing, plug trays are space efficient and effective if you keep a close eye on the plants inside (they are quick to outgrow their plugs and to need more water). Plug trays are available with 220, 162, 128, 98, 50, or 18 cells, each of which houses one seedling. Once seedlings root through the cells, they can be removed easily and transplanted into larger cells, pots, or the garden.

Some suppliers combine many of the features of cell packs and plug trays along with some extras in accelerated, or advanced, propagation systems. These systems combine new technology to make seed starting both

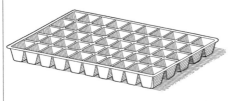

convenient and efficient. One innovation, called the Speedling Transplant Flat, has a grid of pyramidal-shaped cells made of plastic foam. These 3"-deep cells taper down to a point at the base, which is open and allows free air circu-

High-tech propagating flats aerate soils better than plastic cell packs.

lation, great for healthy root growth. Similar to plug trays, plants can be popped out of small cells and transplanted without damage to the roots. Speedling Transplant Flats are available in a variety of cell sizes, from 72 to 300 cells per tray. A version developed for cuttings has 128 openings, 1½" square and 4½" deep.

Propagating sets may be fitted with clear plastic tops or humidity domes, which hold in moist air like a greenhouse, protecting cuttings and seedlings from drying out. Set humidity domes snugly on top of the

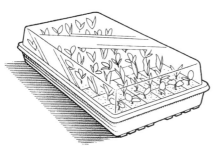

flat for maximum humidity or leave the seal slightly ajar to allow some air circulation. Humidity domes can cost a dollar or more each, but if you take care to stack them carefully when they are not in use, they can last for years.

Humidity domes solve the problems with dry air in heated homes.

Instead of a humidity dome, gardeners can create their own plastic tenting that works the same way but can be made in varying shapes. Humidity tents should be tall enough to allow plant stems to grow straight without touching the plastic, which minimizes foliage disease.

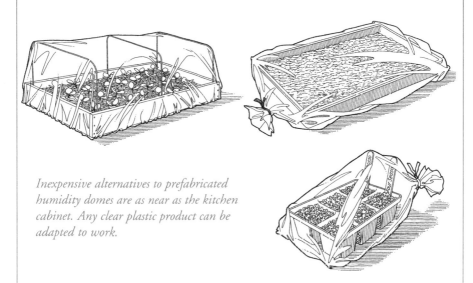

Inexpensive alternatives to prefabricated humidity domes are as near as the kitchen cabinet. Any clear plastic product can be adapted to work.

At the simplest, you can use clear plastic cling wrap to cover pots and flats after sowing seeds. Or you could slide flats into large plastic food storage bags and seal the open end. This will keep moist planting mix damp for a week or more, long enough for many seedlings to germinate and get started. The plastic can stay in place until the seedlings begin to push it up and off. For a humidity tent over a pot, prop up a large, clear plastic kitchen storage bag with a bamboo garden stake held upright inside the edge of the pot.

A more elaborate but still easy alternative is a plastic tunnel. Buy clear plastic sheeting that's thin enough to maneuver easily. Use flexible wire to make arching supports you can set inside a flat or pot to form a tunnel. Cover the arches with the plastic, folding the ends to hold in moisture. As seedlings or cuttings become well established, the ends of the tunnel can be opened to reduce humidity and increase air circulation.

Another great option sometimes included in a complete propagating kit is a wicking or capillary mat, which provides a steady supply of moisture to plug trays, cell packs, or other containers. (For more on commercial and homemade capillary mats, see page 21.) Still other kits may include planting medium, thermometers, labels, and other helpful supplies.

CLAY POTS: Clay, which is blended with other fillers, makes natural-looking brown or reddish brown pots. A clay pot is porous, unlike plastic, and encourages oxygen movement, benefitting cuttings and plants prone to root rot. Clay pots will dry out more quickly than plastic, an advantage in cool, soggy weather but a disadvantage in hot, dry weather. They are heavier than plastic, so they're more stable but less convenient to shuffle around. After a year of use, they may become encrusted with a white coating of salt left from water and fertilizers. Since this residue is capable of damaging plant roots, the pot should be soaked in clear water for an hour and allowed to drain freely when drying to wash off the salts before reuse.

Clay pots come in a variety of sizes, most of which are cylindrical with

Propagating in small clay pots requires more frequent watering than larger pots.

a flaring top, although more decorative types in different shapes, sizes, and ornamentation are available. Clay pots range in size from 1½" to 5" wide at the top—sizes suitable for individual plantings—to 21" or more for large houseplants or patio planters. Cylindrical pots are not as space efficient as square plastic pots but if you buy the same size pots, they will stack into a neat tower when not in use.

The durability of clay pots depends on how they were made and how you handle them. The longest lasting are made with refined clay, which is less likely to chip, and fired at a high temperature to make the pot dark and dense. All clay pots should be stored in a dry place in winter. If left outdoors, they may crack and flake.

Newspaper Pots: Pots for seedlings or cuttings can be made of black-and-white newspaper wrapped around a pot shaper or small jar that is 2½" to 3" in diameter. Cut a 4"-high, 8"-long strip of newspaper, and use it to encircle the cylinder, leaving an inch or more of newspaper extended below the bottom of the cylinder. Fold the extended newspaper together to make a bottom for the pot. You can tape the edges and bottom together or just set the paper pot directly in a flat-bottom flat or tray. Fill the pot with damp, peat-based planting mix and the moisture will make the overlapping newsprint cling together.

This technique may take a few tries to perfect, but soon you will be able to make these pots in less than a minute each, the time spent balancing out the cost of other pots. One potential problem is that newsprint can dry out quickly, which could disrupt root growth, especially when the plants are set outside. They also might fall apart if drenched with a strong stream of water, so they are best kept

When kept moist, newspaper pots make great biodegradable seed starters.

moist with bottom watering or gentle drizzling from above. Plant the young seedling and the paper pot directly in the ground when the time is right. The newsprint will decay in the soil without hindering root growth.

SOIL BLOCKER: A soil blocker is a handy tool that shapes soil into neat cubes with dents in the top for the insertion of a seed. (It requires use of a special live-soil mix described on page 19.) The open-sided blocks are bathed in oxygen from all sides, which can create healthier root systems; however, they tend to dry out quickly. Soil blocks can be planted directly into the ground without disturbing the roots. Blockers, which are made of noncorrosive brass or plastic, cost around twenty dollars. This one-time cost is worthwhile considering the blocker can take decades of hard use.

Soil blockers are available in ¾"- to 4"-cube sizes. The smaller size is adequate for small seeds such as basil and broccoli, but they will also grow nicely in 2"-diameter blocks and will not need to be transplanted as quickly. Two-inch-wide blocks also succeed with large seeds such as pumpkins and squash. An even larger tool can make 4"-wide blocks, ideal for acorns and other tree seeds.

Growing seeds in soil blocks may take some practice. The soil blockers need to be packed firmly with live soil mix (moistened until it clings together and feels like a sponge) to make solid blocks. Once planted, the blocks must be kept out of heavy downpours or they will break up. A good way to gain experience is to experiment with quick-growing seeds such as cucumbers, squash, or pumpkins, which need only a 3-week head start indoors before being transplanted outside.

Start with a blocker that makes 2"-wide cubes. Turn the soil blocker upside down and fill the openings with spongy-moist live soil mix. Press the mix in each opening firmly so that every block will be entirely filled. Then set the blocker inside a flat-bottom flat or tray, and squeeze the soil cubes out of the blocker using the mechanism near the handle. You could put the cubes on a wicking mat, which will keep them evenly moist without overhead watering. Make as many cubes as needed, setting them side by side in the tray.

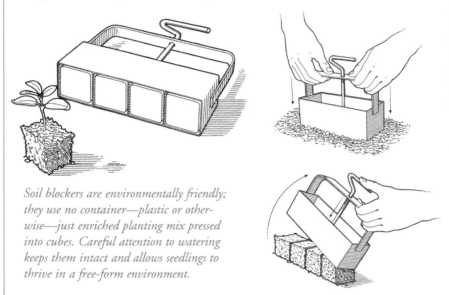

Soil blockers are environmentally friendly; they use no container—plastic or otherwise—just enriched planting mix pressed into cubes. Careful attention to watering keeps them intact and allows seedlings to thrive in a free-form environment.

Slide one seed into each cube and firm the soil mix over the top to cover it. Enclose the flat or tray in a clear plastic bag to retain moisture and put the tray in a warm, bright place. Once the seedlings arise and begin to push against the plastic, remove the bag and be prepared to water—daily if necessary. If no wicking mat is used, moisten the cubes by bottom watering or by using a fine-mist nozzle attached to a watering can. When the seedlings are growing strongly and have rooted through their soil blocks, individual blocks can be carefully separated, scooped up, and transplanted directly into the garden or into a pot.

JIFFY-7 PEAT PELLETS: Jiffy-7 peat pellets are mesh-enclosed cylinders of peat moss, a tidy home for a single seedling. The pellets come in easy-to-store, flat, dry pellets. But when moisture is added, they swell to almost 2" across and over 2" high. There is a neat dent in the top for inserting a seed. Once the seedling is growing and the roots begin to show through the edges of the Jiffy-7, it can be transplanted into a 6" plastic pot or put directly out in the garden. The roots are undisturbed and will not suffer from transplant shock.

If kept in a dry place, Jiffy-7 pellets can be stored for a year or more.

There is a price for this convenience. Jiffy-7 pellets can cost at least twenty cents each, which adds up quickly if you intend to grow a packet of 50 or more seeds. Because the pellets are composed of peat, they do not drain excess moisture as well as other growing mixes and can get overly soggy if watered excessively. The mesh holding the pellet together, although biodegradable, does not always decay during the current growing season and can prevent roots from pushing beyond it into the soil.

PEAT POTS: Peat pots are made of compressed peat moss, formed into individual round or square shapes or strips of connected pots measuring 2", 3", 4", or more across. They cost a nickel or more each and can be used only once. Extra peat pots should be stored in a cool, dry location so they will maintain their shape and will not get stuck to one another.

The main benefit of peat pots is their convenience. The pot changes from medium or dark brown to tan when dry, so it's easy to know when to water. To thoroughly rewet these pots, submerge them in a watering tray for 10 minutes. Peat pots can be transplanted right into the garden when the seedling is ready. The biggest problem with peat pots is that although they are biodegradable, they may not decay reliably in a single season. To alleviate this, use a knife to score the sides and remove the bottom of the pot

Peat pots can be conveniently planted right in the garden.

before planting out so the roots can escape. If the rim of the pot emerges above the soil surface after planting, tear it off or the entire pot could dry out and damage nearby seedling roots.

STERILIZING REUSED EQUIPMENT

Containers can carry spores of diseases harbored in the soil or tissues of the last plant grown in it. For example, bulb pans—low, broad plastic pots that hold forced tulips and hyacinths and can be great for rooting cuttings—may be dusted with microscopic spores of fungus that infected tightly packed and heavily watered bulbs. By sterilizing the pot before reuse, the next crop of cuttings is sure to get off to a healthy start. You also may sterilize pots, flats, cell packs, yogurt cups, milk cartons, and other recycled containers.

Begin by scrubbing the containers well with warm soapy water. Mix a 10% bleach solution (1 part bleach to 9 parts water). Moisten a rag in the bleach solution and wipe the container thoroughly with it. Rinse well. The container is ready to plant.

FIBER PACKS: Inexpensive containers made of brown wood fibers pressed into medium-size 5½" × 7½" × 2¾" packs, fiber packs are convenient to set on a wide windowsill or slip between larger flats in odd openings in a light garden. Seeds or cuttings should always be planted sparingly because no dividers exist to keep roots separated. Although fiber packs can be reused, they are difficult to sterilize and may warp and not stack neatly for storage.

RECYCLED HOUSEHOLD CONTAINERS: Any sturdy, water-holding container that is several inches deep can be used for propagation, including such everyday items as yogurt cups, plastic foam coffee cups, cottage cheese containers, and clear plastic packs from baked goods. When using recycled containers, you should sterilize them and punch holes in the bottom for water drainage.

Consider container shape and size when determining a maintenance program for your propagated plants. Smaller containers will dry out more quickly, requiring extra attention to watering. Square containers, such as the bottoms of 1- or 2-quart milk cartons, can fit together snugly, wasting no space. Low, broad containers, like cottage cheese cartons, are less likely to tip over than tall, narrow containers such as plastic or foam coffee cups, but they also provide less rooting space. A clear plastic bakery or salad bar container, which comes complete with a lid, can double as a mini greenhouse.

PROPAGATION BOXES: Clear plastic utility boxes, sold for packing wool sweaters or storing other goods, make great propagating boxes for cuttings. They are about the same size as a flat but reach 8" or 10" high, providing extra room for stem growth. They have a snug-fitting, clear plastic lid that limits moisture loss. You could plant directly in the box after drilling drainage holes in the bottom, or set pots of cuttings inside.

NURSERY BEDS: Nursery beds are specially adapted places where propagators can start a variety of plants outdoors. The bed, which is a working rather than an ornamental bed, might be put to one side of a vegetable garden or in an out-of-the-way place. It should have full sun (although some cuttings may require shading) and protection from wind. Raise the bed 4"–6" high with naturally rot-resistant cedar or redwood lumber to ensure good drainage. Filling the raised area with well-drained sandy soil or peat-based planting mix will minimize the potential for root rot. Adding an irrigation system will make it easy to water young plants when the weather becomes dry.

SOIL AND POTTING MIXES

Soil and potting mixes, used for propagating plants in containers, provide a home for roots and a place to anchor plants. They are complex environments—a blend of minerals, organic material, air, moisture, and (for soil or live soil mixes) a microscopic community of subterranean life.

In a garden, where you might sow zinnia or bean seeds directly in the earth, soil is composed of varying mineral elements. Sandy soil, which has a large percentage of coarse sand, tends to be loose and well drained but also dry and low in nutrients. Clay soil, with abundant fine-textured clay, can be tight and stiff, low in oxygen, sometimes poorly drained and easily waterlogged. Both of these

STERILE MIX RECIPES

PEAT-BASED SEED STARTING MIX:
1 part milled Canadian sphagnum peat moss with 1 part perlite or vermiculite.

PEAT-BASED PLANTING MIX:
1 part milled Canadian sphagnum peat moss with 1 part horticultural vermiculite and 1 part coarse sand or perlite.

FERTILIZER

Live-soil mixes and organic-rich soils may contain all the nutrients young plants need to begin their lives. But peat-based mixes and Jiffy-7 peat pellets, which contain little or no nutrients, may require the addition of fertilizers, especially after seedlings have grown in them for more than 6 weeks or when cuttings begin to root.

Fertilizers can contain one or more nutrients. Macronutrients, required by all plants, include nitrogen, which stimulates growth; phosphorus, which encourages good root and fruit development; and potassium, vital for good health. These elements are identified on fertilizer labels by a ratio indicating the percentages of nitrogen, phosphorus, and potassium.

Micronutrients, necessary only in tiny amounts, include magnesium, manganese, calcium, copper, boron, sulfur, and others that play small but vital roles in plant metabolism. They generally are abundant in organic-rich soil and compost but often are missing from synthetic fertilizers.

Organic fertilizers, made from natural sources, generally contain low levels of nutrients and release them slowly, providing gentle, non-burning fertilization. They help beneficial soil microorganisms and will not pollute. Here are a few common organic fertilizers suitable for using after propagating.

Smith and Hawken granular fertilizers for tomatoes and vegetables are blended from bonemeal, blood meal, fish meal, alfalfa, cottonseed meal, kelp, and rock phosphate. They contain 4% nitrogen, 5% phosphorus, and 2% potassium.

Bat guano, which stimulates leafy growth, contains 10% nitrogen, 4% phosphorus, and 1% potassium.

Bonemeal, good for root and bulb development, contains 2% nitrogen, 11% phosphorus, and 22% calcium.

Cottonseed meal, a slow-release fertilizer for plants such as rhododendrons that prefer acid soils, has 7% nitrogen, 2% phosphorus, and 2% potassium.

extreme soil types and more moderate soils that blend sand and clay with other mineral elements, can be improved with the addition of organic matter.

Organic matter—compost, decayed leaves or wood, rotted stable manure and straw—enriches sand, helping it stay moist and supplying a gentle flow of nutrients. Organic matter in heavy clay soils breaks up compacted molecules and clumps fine particles into larger aggregates, creating a porous texture suitable for air movement and water drainage.

Soils need to contain at least 5% organic matter to benefit from it. Less than ideal soils are improved if they have 10% or more organic matter. For new beds, this means working a layer of compost several inches deep into the soil. Adding another couple of inches of compost or other organic material as mulch every following year will help maintain desirable levels of organic material.

True soil has been replaced by peat-based planting mixes as the medium of choice for propagating and, in general, for growing potted plants. They are sterile and provide a good balance of water and oxygen. The blended mixes hold moisture but quickly shed any excess water, leaving open pore space where air can penetrate. However, if peat-based mixes are allowed to dry out, they can be hard to moisten thoroughly again. Bottom watering is a good remedy. When perfectly moist—neither too wet nor too dry—these mixes will hold together like a soft sponge, an ideal condition for good seed germination and plant growth. (In contrast, true soil can harbor insect pests and diseases that attack young seedlings or cuttings. It also can compress, packing down when watered until it becomes too dense for good root growth or free water and air movement.)

For gardeners who start only a couple of cuttings or seedlings each year, a small bag of peat-based mix will be sufficient. Avid propagators can buy large bags (2½ cubic feet) that last longer and cost less per cubic foot than smaller bags. If you find a discount source of peat and perlite or vermiculite (common contents of peat-based mixes), you may be able to make your own potting mixes for less than the retail cost of pre-made peat blends. Organic gardeners may want to make their own mix to be certain it contains no nonorganic fertilizers.

LIVE-SOIL MIX: If you are using a soil blocker (described on page 13), peat-based mixes must be

> ## LIVE-SOIL MIX RECIPES
>
> **LIGHT LIVE SOIL:** 3 parts peat-based mix with 1 part compost.
> **HEAVY LIVE SOIL:** 1 part compost with 1 part vermiculite.

modified with compost to make a live-soil mix. Live soil is thicker and richer, clinging more securely into a block. It is also good for

MAKING HOT COMPOST

Yard and kitchen scraps can become a great soil amendment and propagating tool. A pile of fallen leaves, seedless weeds, vegetable leaves—even old coffee grounds—in an out-of-the-way corner of your yard will eventually decay into compost. This gradual decay process is called cold composting and results in a useful garden additive but a less than ideal component for propagating mixes. Cold compost could harbor disease spores and weed seeds that will overwhelm young seedlings or cuttings.

A better way to make compost for live-soil propagating mixes is by hot composting. This requires blending nitrogen-rich, soft, green foliage or livestock manures with hard, brown, carbon-rich material like straw, wood shavings, and fallen leaves. The combination provides a balance of nutrients that microorganisms prefer to feed on, thus decomposing the material quickly. When plenty of air is added, decomposition accelerates to the point that it generates heat that can destroy weed seeds, diseases, and pests.

The easiest way to produce hot compost is to buy a composting system. Various bins, barrels, and tubs have been developed to spin or whirl green and brown matter, providing ideal aeration and inciting rapid decay of materials.

More traditional methods of producing hot compost involve making a compost pile. Lay sturdy twigs on the ground in a 3-foot-square composting area. (The twigs allow some air penetration through the bottom of the pile.) Make an organic sandwich, layering 4" of shredded brown material and 2" of green material to make the pile 3' high. Use a composting or garden fork to fluff and turn the pile as often as every 3 weeks, aerating it in the process. When all the material has turned into fluffy brown compost—leaving its original identity in doubt—it is ready for use in a live-soil mix.

growing transplanted seedlings, rooted cuttings, and small divisions or layered stems. Because compost may not be sterile and could harbor bacteria and fungi, it is best to use hot compost, which has decayed rapidly, to generate heat that kills pathogens and weed seeds. Work homemade compost through a screen to break up large clumps and remove twigs. If you don't have a compost pile at home, try bagged composted cow manure, which may be sterilized before it is packaged.

Watering

Water is a vital element for all living things, plants included, and it should be handled with care when propagating. Most seedlings, cuttings, new divisions, and layered plants need to be kept evenly moist and will not tolerate drying out or being oversaturated. For this reason, it is important to keep good watering equipment on hand. An ordinary garden hose, sprinkler, or watering can are not the only options for watering propagated plants.

BOTTOM WATERING: Flats and pots of plants can be watered from the bottom by sitting propagating containers in flats of water and letting the planting medium soak up the moisture. Remove the pots and flats once they are moist and let them drain freely to eliminate excess water.

Bottom watering is the least disruptive way to water seedlings.

WATER WAND: Water wands, which can be screwed onto the end of a hose, have a fine-spray head that softens the flow of water so it will not damage soil, small seedlings, or cuttings. Wands are set on long metal handles that make them easy to maneuver into any spot, even hanging baskets.

RUBBER SPRINKLER: For very fine seeds, young seedlings, or soil cubes, a rubber bulbous hand sprinkler provides moisture in the gentlest fashion. It can be filled with 12 ounces of water and lightly squeezed to let water flow over the seedlings.

WICKING OR CAPILLARY MAT: This is a water-absorbent sheet of fabric, that, like a sponge, can soak up water from a nearby reservoir and supply it to plants. The mat can be set beneath flats, plug trays, peat pots, Jiffy-7s, soil cubes, or any propagating container with openings in the bottom. You can buy high-tech mats from garden suppliers or make your own with double-knit jersey cloth folded in a double layer and set

MOISTENING PLANTING MEDIUM

It is always best to have the planting medium slightly moist when you sow seeds or plant. Planted dry, a pot filled with peat-based planting mix is next to impossible to moisten thoroughly. If you don't mind a little mess, and you need to moisten a lot of mix at once, do it in a dishpan, bucket, or even a wheelbarrow. Keep adding small amounts of water and mix thoroughly—get in there and use your hands—until the mixture is uniformly damp, not wet. For small amounts, a zipper-seal plastic bag works well. Add about 1 part water to 4 parts mix; seal the bag and gently knead it until the water is uniformly incorporated in the mix.

on plastic beneath the propagation unit. Fill a plastic jug with water and make a hole in the cap. Upend the jug on the fabric so the water slowly trickles out, keeping the cloth evenly moist.

If you are starting plants in a pot, you can purchase self-watering pots with self-contained wicking systems. Slender wicks emerge from the base of the planting area and dangle down into a moisture reservoir, drawing up water as the planting mix above dries out.

MISTING: Sometimes cuttings or newly transplanted seedlings will wilt from lack of roots and too much demand for moisture. To reduce water stress, you can mist the foliage with a handheld mister. This process should be repeated often—every hour if possible. Or look for a mist propagation unit. Some specialty garden catalogs sell clear propagating boxes, some with their own heating and lighting attachments, that also automatically fill with mist at regular intervals.

DRIP AND TRICKLE IRRIGATION: Overhead sprinkling, which lets large drops of water fly like bombs from a cannon onto tiny seeds, waters indiscriminately—catching weeds, walks, chairs, and people. A better way to handle watering is with drip or trickle irrigation that gently emits droplets of moisture at ground level and only to specific target plants. Plant foliage remains dry, which discourages foliage diseases. Once assembled, these systems can be run on timers. Drip or trickle irrigation systems call for a series of water-carrying lines to be laid through the garden. For vegetable gardens, simple soaker hosing can run straight up the middle of rows and keep germinating seeds and transplanted seedlings moist.

For ornamental gardens, flexible plastic tubing with moisture emitters tailored to the soil and plant needs can honeycomb the area and be hidden beneath mulch. Emitters can be hooked up to propagating flats and potted plants to keep them moist.

LIGHTING

Plants, which lie at the bottom of the food chain, form the foundation of life by capturing sunlight and converting it into sugars by the process of photosynthesis. Every plant needs light to grow, but the intensity of light required varies according to the plant. Most grasses, vegetables, such as tomatoes and broccoli, and flowers, such as peonies and poppies, need full sun—at least 6 hours a day. Other plants, such as mints, bleeding heart, hydrangeas, rhododendrons, and flowering dogwood do better in light shade, 4 to 6 hours of sun a day. A few plants, including English ivy and pachysandra, grow well in full shade, with less than 4 hours of sun a day.

Young cuttings and seedlings need varying levels of light, depending on how strong their root systems are. Young plants with well-developed roots can grow in full light (the maximum amount the species prefers), which encourages active photosynthesis and maximum growth but can also increase the chance of wilting. Cuttings with few or no roots need minimal light to prevent moisture loss until their roots develop.

When propagating outdoors, you can put potted plants in full sun or shade, according to their needs. If plants are started in nursery beds or cold frames (described on page 27), you can cover the growing area with shade cloth, designed in varying densities to screen out different amounts of sunlight. There are several ways to provide light indoors.

WINDOWSILL: In climates with reliably sunny weather, a windowsill may provide sufficient light for seedlings and other propagated plants, especially plants such as squash, basil, and sunflowers, that need only a short head start indoors. Assuming windows are not shaded by evergreens or eaves, south-facing windows will be brightest and make the best choice for sun-loving plants. East- or west-facing windows, which receive only half a day of sun, may suffice for well-rooted sun-lovers. Bright north-facing windows—if they are not deeply cast in shadows all day—receive no direct sun and can work well for new cuttings that have not yet established roots.

LIGHT GARDEN: This is a growing space illuminated with electric light to replace or supplement sunlight. In areas with cloudy weather in winter and early spring—times when seedlings and cuttings depend on bright light to get off to a strong start—a light garden makes a good alternative to windowsill gardening. You can purchase prefabricated light gardens with several sets of shelves, each illuminated with a pair of overhead lightbulbs. A homemade alternative is a simple two-tube fluorescent light fixture hung over a table on adjustable-length chains or ropes.

Several kinds of lightbulbs are suitable for light gardening but

cool fluorescent bulbs are best for seedlings and cuttings. The only shortcoming is their limited light intensity, well below that of natural sunlight. For this reason, it is important to make the most of what light is available.

Set the lightbulbs just 1"–2" above the seedlings. (Fluorescent lights stay cool and seldom burn leaves, even if in direct contact.)

One way to ensure good results when propagating is to use fluorescent lights.

The seedlings closest to the center of the tubes will receive more light than those near the end. This can be remedied by rotating the plants. Lining nearby walls with aluminum foil will help to reflect stray light back to the seedlings. Plug the lights into an automatic timer, set to turn on the lights for 14 to 16 hours a day, which adds up to a reasonable approximation of sun exposure. The timer, which is really the best asset for any beginning seed-starter because doing it manually is tough to maintain consistency, will turn the lights off at night. If the seedlings look a little lanky, you can leave the lights on an hour or two longer.

Labeling

Since many plants look similar when young, it is vital to have a labeling system. This can be done in a variety of ways. When dividing perennials out in the garden, you can avoid using obtrusive labels by keeping track of your plants on a garden plan. One way to do this is with garden design software, which is easy to update every time you divide a daylily and set more clumps in a new location. A simpler way to keep track of your plantings is by hand. Sketch your garden plantings in pencil so you can erase and adapt as the design changes.

Some gardeners find it easier to use labels that can be inserted into the ground beside the plant. This is usually not objectionable for vegetable gardens. In ornamental gardens, where utilitarian tags might ruin the aesthetic appeal, decorative labels of stone or ceramic might suffice.

But when it comes to seedlings, labeling is an absolute necessity. Label each row with a marker that names the plant and gives the date seeded. Leave space for adding germination time or date of transplantation. When sowing indoors or out, mark and label the seed rows with indelible ink or pencil on garden stakes, small, flat wooden sticks, or anything else that does the job.

Plastic Labels: White, green, yellow, and red plastic labels, available in 4", 6", 8", or 12" lengths, are a standard in nurseries and easily available for home gardeners. They are inexpensive—just pennies each if bought in bulk—but not particularly attractive or long-lasting. Write the plant name on the tag, using marking pencil or permanent marker, but do not be surprised if it fades in several months. The tags also are prone to breaking or shifting out of place and getting lost, leaving little clue to the name of the plant they were meant to identify.

For marking rows of seedlings or cuttings in flats or making temporary labels of outdoor sown seedlings, you could replace horticultural tags with recycled kitchen plastics—anything large enough to write a plant name on. Used plastic spoons and knives, plastic milk or water cartons cut into strips, or sections of plastic foam vegetable trays will all work. Plan to upgrade to more permanent labels once the seedlings go outdoors.

WOODEN LABELS: Many gardeners prefer wooden tags to plastic ones. They are less likely to break and look more natural in the garden. If they get buried by a passing rototiller, they will decompose and improve the soil, unlike plastic tags.

METAL LABELS: These are shiny aluminum or zinc tags set on long-legged stakes that will stay put in the garden. Write plant names on the tags with a ballpoint pen, which dents the metal, leaving the letters etched into the tag. When the ink washes off, the tag still does its job. Metal labels are highly visible, but you may be able to position them amid foliage so their impact is reduced.

STONE LABELS: You could make your own labels on flat pieces of stone, using outdoor paint—the color of your choice—to print the plant name on the stone. They will look natural but will not be securely anchored and may be moved unintentionally.

CERAMIC LABELS: An abundance of artistic-looking ceramic plant labels can be found at garden centers, nurseries, gift shops, or even department stores. These often have a long ceramic base, suitable for inserting into the soil, and a decorative shape with the common name indicated at the top. Ceramic labels are attractive, but generally are not sturdy and will not hold up to unintentional whacks with a hoe or freezing winter weather. They usually come with only generic plant names—thyme, beans, poppy—and cannot be used to designate more specific botanical or cultivar names.

TEMPERATURE CONTROL

Plants are at their most fragile during infancy periods of seed growth or stem cutting. In this stage, the temperature of their soil and surroundings is critical. There are many marvelous devices—for indoors and outside—at the gardener's disposal. Sometimes all a seedling needs is a windowsill, a warm place above the refrigerator, or a dehumidifier, but other times more wonderfully ingenious equipment such as a heating cable or the Wall O' Water is necessary.

INDOORS: When starting plants indoors, you may be able to find a range of temperatures around your house that will be suitable for particular propagation projects. A basement or an unheated spare room may stay around 60°F in the winter, great for starting seeds of cool-season crops. In the same house, the top of the refrigerator or a spot beside a sunny south-facing window may stay 75° or 80°F, which is perfect for starting many kinds of annual flower seeds. If no natural warm spot exists, you can make one with heating cables.

HEATING CABLES: Gardeners who start warmth-loving plants from cuttings or seed like chili peppers that germinate best at about 80°F—will love heating cables. These are insulated cables that can be laid in the bottom of flats or trays, providing extra warmth to cell packs, plug trays, flats of Jiffy-7s, or soil blocks that are set inside. Giving cuttings or seedlings a dose of tropical bottom heat will encourage rapid growth. Depending on the make, heating cables may warm areas 15° or 20°F above the ambient temperature or they may be preset to maintain a certain temperature.

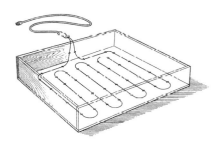

Heating cables take the guesswork out of germinating warm-season plants.

If making a heating tray from heating cables is too time-consuming, you can buy preassembled heating mats. One heavy-duty propagation mat is made of rubber and can adjust to provide temperatures from 40° to 100°F. Another brand comes with a wire flat-holding rack to set above the heating mat so the flat is bathed in rising warm air.

OUTDOORS: If propagating outside, timing and season will determine the prevailing temperature, although cold can be moderated with cold frames, floating row covers, cloches, Wall O' Waters, and protected tunnels.

COLD FRAME: Cold frames are clear plastic-, glass-, or fiberglass-encased growth chambers set on top of the ground. They rely on heat from the sun and the elimination of wind to protect dormant or semi-evergreen cuttings and divisions taken in late fall from excessive winter cold. They are also ideal for storing potted daffodils to bring indoors and force for extra-early bloom. In late winter or early spring,

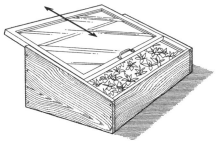

Cold frames come in many different sizes and styles, with something appropriate for every yard.

they can give an outdoor head start to newly sprouted root cuttings or seedlings of spring vegetables such as cabbages or onions. In fall, they can be planted with seeds of lettuce, arugula, spinach, and other greens to provide salad harvests deep into winter.

Gardeners can plant directly in cold frames, filling them with coarse sand for rooting cuttings or rich soil for salad greens. Cold frames can also be filled with container-grown plants, transferring them in and out of shelter as needed.

Cold frames work best if they are higher in the back than in the front and have the transparent top angled to the south to catch maximum sunshine. They can be 3' high, which allows enough growing room for most seedlings, cuttings, and divisions, and no more than 4' wide so they are easy to reach into and maintain. For maximum light and heat, a cold frame can be set against a light-colored, south-facing wall.

There are many different kinds of cold frames. Traditional ones, used in past decades, have a cement-block base with glass windowpanes forming a greenhouse-like top. They are well-insulated but cumbersome arrangements. A temporary and inexpensive homemade cold frame can be assembled from four hay bales set in a square and covered with a window sash.

Contemporary cold frames, available in easy-to-assemble kits, have rectangular metal frames and lightweight insulated plastic or fiberglass walls and tops. Some come with automatic openers that raise the hinged top when the inside temperature reaches about 75°F. This protects cuttings and seedlings from overheating and wilting. A low-maintenance gardener can combine this feature with trickle irrigation or capillary matting to tend to the watering.

HOT FRAME: Before the advent of greenhouses, American pioneers grew vitamin-rich greens during winter in hot frames. Today, a hot frame is easily made by winding insulated, moisture-proof heating cables in the bottom of a cold frame.

Before electric heating cables, frames were warmed with livestock manure. When manure decomposes, it heats up, which is why a manure mound will steam on a cool spring morning. The best manures for heat come from chickens, cows, and horses. Collect what fresh manure you can and let it begin to decompose in your compost pile. After several weeks or when it begins to cool, it will be ripe for the hot frame. Dig a hole 3' deep in the cold frame and set in a 2'-deep layer of the decomposing manure. Cover with a foot of topsoil or sand and let the hot bed rest for several more weeks if the manure emits too much heat. To avoid burning the plants inside, don't plant until the temperature drops below 85°F, then enjoy this natural source of pollution-free heat.

FLOATING ROW COVERS: These are lightweight fabrics that can be set directly on plants and pinned to the ground nearby, raising the interior ambient temperature several degrees. When you start seedlings extraearly outdoors, double up floating row covers for extra frost protection. Single layers are fine for germinating seeds, starting cuttings, or growing plants after propagating them.

Floating row covers allow sun, moisture, and air to penetrate to plants below and have the added attraction of keeping out flying insects. With the exception of onions, plants will grow freely beneath the fabric, pushing it up as they grow—hence the name floating row cover. (Onion leaves, delicate hollow tubes, are not strong enough to do this, even with ultra-lightweight row covers. They need some supportive hoops or props to hold the covers up for them but benefit greatly from the frost protection row covers can provide in early spring.)

PROTECTED TUNNELS: These are like temporary greenhouses, constructed right out in the garden over a bed of seedlings, divisions, or cuttings that need special frost protection. Tunnel kits come complete with wire hoops to set over the plants and greenhouse-quality plastic or heavy-duty row covers to stretch over the hoops. The plastic or row covers can clip onto the supports or merely rest on them and be secured to the ground with metal earth staples, soil, rocks, or bricks.

Put your croquet wickets to good use by making propagating tunnels.

Do-it-yourselfers can make their own tunnels with 10-gage galvanized steel wire, cut long enough to bury the ends a foot deep and still leave some growing space for plants inside the tunnel. Set the wire hoops 5'–8' apart and cover them with plastic or row covers.

Plastic tunnels, which get warmer on sunny days than row covers, will need to be removed before the weather becomes hot. Heavy-duty row covers, such as Tufbell, do not encourage as much heat buildup and can give reasonable frost protection. Tufbell, for instance, absorbs mois-

A dome tunnel for an individual plant.

Wall O' Water protectors are extra insulation.

ture, and if the temperature drops below freezing, will form a shield of ice to protect the plants below.

CLOCHES: In centuries gone, glass bell jars were inverted over tender plants to protect them from frost and cold. The glass trapped sunlight to warm the air inside and held in humidity, which benefitted cuttings, divisions, and other plants establishing new roots.

Contemporary cloches take many forms but are designed to protect a single plant. Cylinders, domes, umbrellas, or rectangles of clear or transparent colored plastic, often with perforated tops for air circulation, can be set over seedlings or rooted cuttings planted outdoors during cool weather.

WALL O' WATER: A ring of water-filled tubes forms a clear, aquatic teepee around a garden plant, keeping off all but the most severe frost. In garden trials, tender vegetables such as tomatoes have survived outdoors in a Wall O' Water down to 16°F. Water, the key to the exceptional performance, absorbs the heat of the sun during the day and holds that heat late into the night when temperatures are likely to get the coldest. Because the cylinders are clear, sunlight continues to penetrate to the plant below but rainfall may be kept out. Seedlings or rooted cuttings kept under a Wall O' Water for several weeks or more should be checked for adequate moisture every few days and watered individually if necessary.

SEEDS

Seeds, the product of sexual reproduction, are young plant embryos encased in a protective seed coat. They are capable of lying dormant—for a year or many years depending on the species—until conditions are right for germination, the initiation of growth, and subsequent seedling emergence from the seed.

Because they are small, inexpensive, and able to be packaged, stored, and transported with ultimate ease, seeds are a handy method of propagation for the gardener. They can be purchased at a store or through the mail, kept in a corner of a shelf or drawer until the growing season approaches, then allowed to grow and flourish. Many choice species and cultivars become available to the propagator willing to invest time in seed sowing.

There are thousands of different kinds of seeds, which range from easy to complex to sow. Some need special treatments to sprout. Most need some nurturing early on, but the length of the protective period required varies from species to species. Quick-growing annuals such as basil and zinnias are a snap to sow directly in the garden soil. They arise within days and may be flowering within 6 to 8 weeks. Others, such as slow-starting perennials, shrubs, or trees, can take months to germinate and a year or more of supervision to reach self-sustaining maturity.

How similar seedlings will be to siblings from the same packet of seeds depends on whether they are hybrid or open-pollinated. If started from commercial hybrid cultivars, cultivated lines of seeds bred from dissimilar parent plants for a special blend of their characteristics, the seedlings will grow into startlingly similar plants. If grown from open-pollinated seeds, the offspring can grow into a similar but not identical group of siblings, which is perfectly acceptable for an informal garden.

SEEDS IN NATURE

The ability of plants to encapsulate their offspring in seed coats and protect them, sometimes for years on end, is a lifesaver for the species. When winter cold, killing drought, fire, or other natural catastrophes arise, the species' offspring can be protected. The closed-cone pines of the western United States, for instance, require exposure to fire to release their seeds, quickly colonizing the fire-stripped area.

Seeds also give ordinarily immobile plants wings to fly and feet to walk. Dandelion seeds have plumes that can ride the wind high into the sky. Dust-fine orchid seeds are so light that air currents can carry them for hundreds of miles before lowering them to the ground. Buoyant and water-tight coconuts, which are also seeds, float across the high seas and wash up on friendly beaches. They can quickly colonize large areas of beachfront. Seeds may be surrounded with sweet, juicy, or colorful fruit to attract animals who eat the fruits, then travel around the countryside. They emit the seeds in their droppings, providing a fertilized home for the young seedlings.

All seeds carry stored food within the seed coat that can sustain the seedlings as they rise through the soil to the sunny surface. But beyond that point, most seedlings are on their own and entirely dependent on you to provide the light and fertilizer they need in order to thrive. Their small root systems and tender leaves make them vulnerable to any stress—dry soil, too much or too little sun, drying winds, animals, and pathogens. You must plan ahead to avoid these problems if your crop is to be established successfully.

SEED STRUCTURE

A seed, like a hen's egg, contains everything necessary to create a new life. There is an embryo of a baby plant, stored food, and a seed coat that binds it all in a neat package. The different size and makeup of these characteristics account for the differences in germination time, planting depth, and special treatments that may be necessary to speed germination and early seedling growth.

Embryos, fledgling plants held within seeds, resemble a short section of stem with meristems, or growth centers, at both ends. One meristem produces new shoots and the other produces new roots that push out from the seed as it begins to germinate.

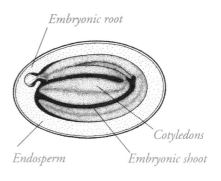

Embryonic root

Cotyledons

Endosperm

Embryonic shoot

Cotyledons, also called seed leaves, are located within the seed and have a different shape than the true leaves that arise once the seedling begins growing. They hold stored endosperm, food made up primarily of starches and proteins. The embryo can draw on the nutrition within the cotyledons until its true leaves begin producing their own food. Cotyledons are easy to observe in bean seedlings. When the young bean sprout emerges from the soil, it carries two plump, round cotyledons low on the stem. They remain prominent on the seedling until the true

leaves—identifiable by a characteristic heart shape—expand. Then the cotyledons shrivel and disappear, their job complete.

Larger seeds, which generally carry more endosperm, are suitable for deeper planting. Edible seeds such as coconuts have huge quantities of endosperm—which makes up both the milk and the meat of the coconut. Other seeds that have an edible endosperm include corn, wheat, peas, beans, and sunflowers.

Small seeds such as orchids, petunias, and rhododendrons are very fine. They have little endosperm and need to be dusted on or just under the surface of the soil to be able to germinate.

THE DIFFERENCE BETWEEN MONOCOTS AND DICOTS

Monocotyledons and dicotyledons—two anatomically distinct types of seeds—represent two lines of evolution. Monocotyledons include corn, grasses, lilies, and other nonwoody plants with parallel veins in the leaves. All are similar in that the seeds contain only one seed leaf or cotyledon.

Dicotyledons, alternatively, have two seed leaves. They include plants such as begonias, coralbells, elms, hydrangeas, maples, oaks, and viburnums. Dicotyledons mostly have netted leaf veins, many are woody, and all have dual seed leaves.

The seed coat encloses and protects the embryo. Coats of seeds such as wisteria and smokebush are very hard and may need special treatments to soften the seed coats before germination. Others, such as corn or pea seeds, are not armor-coated and are quick to germinate when conditions are right.

FLOWER STRUCTURE

Although they occur on most of the plants in existence today, flowers and seeds are a relatively new feature on the historical time line. Around the time that dinosaurs became extinct, there arose a group of plants called angiosperms, plants with seeds borne within a fruit. The protected seeds originated when leaves became folded around reproductive organs, forming flowers and then pods, capsules, and other fruits. Other surrounding leaves were modified—given bright colors and fragrances that would attract bees and other pollinators. The flower was borne.

Sexual organs within flowers are responsible for producing seeds. They are broken down into female and male counterparts. The production of seeds occurs within the pistil, the female part of the plant, which in some flowers is a bowling-pin-shaped structure composed of several parts and located in the center of the blossom. The ovary, located at the base of the pistil, contains one, several, or many ovules, which hold half of the genetic content of the flower and will combine with pollen to become seeds. The stigma, or the tip of the pistil, accepts genetically compatible pollen and allows it to germinate in a process called pollination. Pollen tubes carry pollen down through the pistil into the ovary to fertilize the ovules in a process called fertilization.

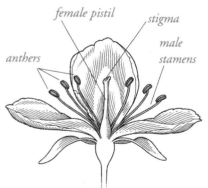

female pistil *stigma*
male stamens
anthers

The stamens, or male portion of the flower, often protrude with rings of filaments located near the center of the flower. With spider flowers (*Cleome* spp.), the long-legged stamens are prominent, easily recognizable, and part of the ornamental charm of the flower. Stamens terminate in lobed anthers, chambers that hold the pollen that harbors the other half of the genetic component of new seeds. When ripe, the anthers break down and the pollen is carried by wind or pollinating insects to the flower stigma, the beginning of the pollination process.

TIPS AND TECHNOLOGY

Understanding seed biology and how it affects germination, as well as knowing how to evaluate seed from different sources, provides a strong start for seed propagators.

SEED GERMINATION: To begin germinating, all seeds need a balanced blend of three basic elements—moisture, oxygen, and temperature. Some also require light.

MOISTURE: Dormant seeds contain little moisture—much less than growing plants—which helps keep them in suspended animation. Some dormant seeds contain only 5% moisture by weight, increasing to as much as 80% when they are ready to germinate. The seed actually swells, a phenomenon easily observed when soaking dried peas or beans in water overnight. This rapid rise in moisture levels, a process called imbibition, marks the start of germination. It activates enzymes that allow the embryo to use the stored food within the seed to begin growing.

Moisture remains important throughout germination and while the young seedling is becoming established. If germinating seeds or seedlings are allowed to dry out, they are likely to die. Parsnips, for instance, need several weeks in moist soil to germinate. If the soil dries out at any time during that germination period, the seeds will not grow.

OXYGEN: In addition to moisture, seeds need oxygen to use stored food supplies. This is not as simple as it sounds because oxygen and water compete for pore space between coarse soil particles. Too much of a good thing—water—can saturate the soil, leaving no room for oxygen. Seeds will rot instead of sprout. If the soil is allowed to dry out, it will be well aerated but not moist enough for germination. Achieving an ideal balance between oxygen and water calls for careful watering, using containers with drainage holes in the bottom, and planting in well-drained, peat-based seed-starting mixes (described on page 17).

TEMPERATURE: The temperature regulates when seeds begin to absorb moisture and use oxygen to grow. Cold temperatures keep seeds dormant. Warmer temperatures encourage germination. But the ideal germination temperature varies according to the plant.

Plants such as lettuce and spinach, called cool-season plants, grow well in cool weather and begin to germinate when temperatures reach 55° to 65°F. They will not germinate well in summer when temperatures are over 85°F. Warm-season plants such as basil and peppers need warmer soils—70° to 80°F—to germinate well.

When sowing seeds outdoors, the time of the year usually determines soil temperatures. Cool-season crops generally are planted 4 to 6 weeks before the last spring frost date or when soils are moderately cool but not cold. Warm-season crops should not be planted until after the last frost date, or even several weeks after that in cold climates, so that the soil is thoroughly warm. Experienced gardeners may be able to feel the soil and evaluate its temperature fairly accurately or they may use a soil thermometer for a more exact measurement.

LIGHT: Small seeds, seeds sown at relatively cool temperatures, and crops such as lettuce, wax begonias, and browallia may need light to germinate. Light tells the seed that it is near enough to the soil surface to be able to emerge and become self-supporting with the limited food reserves held within. If a seed packet says to sprinkle the seed on the surface of the soil, the seed may very well require light. In that case, it is helpful to cover a peat-based seed-starting mix with a thin layer of perlite or vermiculite, which allows more light penetration than the planting mix. Press the seeds shallowly into this surface layer and keep the container in a well-lit spot.

Light levels can be manipulated to prevent germination. Light encourages the sprouting of many kinds of weed seeds lying dormant in the soil. Mulching gardens, covering the soil with sunlight-blocking layers of material such as shredded bark or straw, dramatically reduces weed germination.

GERMINATION ENHANCEMENT: Seeds have intricate mechanisms for determining whether the time and place is right for sprouting. Learning what conditions seeds need to break their dormancy is necessary for success with this form of propagation.

Seeds from cold or dry climates often have a dormant, or resting, period to protect them during weather that is unsuitable for growth. If seeds of hardy plants take until late summer or autumn to mature, they generally rest through the winter to emerge in spring. Some plants ensure their seeds will not grow prematurely—during a brief warm spell in mid winter, for instance—by requiring a period of after ripening or further development of the embryo during cold-weather dormancy. Other seeds contain chemicals that prevent growth until spring rains (or similar moist conditions) penetrate the seed coat and dissolve the chemical growth inhibitors.

Both dormancy mechanisms can be overcome by planting the seeds in the autumn and leaving them outdoors during the winter to experience

SEEDS REQUIRING STRATIFICATION

Some seeds will germinate only after they have been exposed to several months of continuous cold, usually between 32° and 45°F. In nature, winter provides the chill. You can simulate winter by covering the seeds with damp peat moss and refrigerating them for the specified time.

NAME	CHILLING TIME
Barberries (*Berberis* spp.)	1–3 months
Blazing stars (*Liatris* spp.)	4 weeks
Bleeding heart (*Dicentra spectabilis*)	6 weeks
Clematis (*Clematis* spp.)	3 months
Columbines (*Aquilegia* spp.)	3 weeks
Daylilies (*Hemerocallis* spp.)	6 weeks
Firs (*Abies* spp.)	2–3 months
Honeysuckle (*Lonicera* spp.)	1–2 months
Hornbeams (*Carpinus* spp.)	3–4 months
Lilacs (*Syringa* spp.)	1–3 months
Lobelias (*Lobelia* spp.)	12 weeks
Maples (*Acer* spp.)	2–4 months
Monkshood (*Acontinum carmichaelii*)	3 weeks
Primroses (*Primula* spp.)	4 weeks
Roses (*Rosa* spp.)	4–5 months

normal cold cycles and germinate naturally. Coaxing some seeds into growth earlier indoors can require special treatments such as stratification, scarification, and presoaking.

STRATIFICATION: Refrigerating seeds to provide a cold, moist period similar to winter can fulfill the dormancy requirements of hardy trees and shrubs such as beeches, birches, and maples as well as perennials such as angelica, garden phlox, gas plant, and roses.

The easiest way to accomplish stratification is to preplant seeds in a small 4" or 6" pot, so they can begin growing as soon as the cold requirement has been fulfilled. Fill a sterile pot with lightly moistened peat-based seed-starting mix and plant the seeds within it as indicated on the seed packet. Enclose the pot in a clear plastic bag and seal it. Set the bagged pot in your refrigerator for the time required by the species planted, which may be indicated on the seed packet. Many stratification-requiring annuals and perennials need 6 weeks of cold; many hardy trees and shrubs need 3 months or more of cold. When the cold period has been fulfilled, remove the pot and put it in a warm and bright place for good seedling growth.

SCARIFICATION: Seeds of black locust, camellia, cotoneaster, golden-rain tree, honey locust, redbud, tree peony, and other species have hard, armored seed coats. These seed coats are so sturdy that they may not allow moisture to penetrate the seed and initiate germination. Nick or chip large seeds (like *Wisteria* spp.) with a sharp knife, removing a small sliver from the end of the seed. Or rub the ends of large seeds with sand-

paper. Place small seeds in a jar lined with coarse sandpaper, cover and shake vigorously to scarify them. Plant the seeds immediately; they cannot remain dormant without their protective seed coats intact.

A few seeds require nicking to allow moisture to penetrate the seed coat.

PRESOAKING: As a rule, presoaking seed in tepid to hot water overnight before sowing encourages rapid germination. Presoaking is necessary for seeds with chemical inhibitors that must be leached out before sowing and is recommended for larger, thick-coated seeds like parsley (*Petroselinum*) and sweet peas (*Lathyrus odoratus*). Soaking seeds of trees such as redbud and honey locust mimics the spring rains that soften the seed coat in nature.

EVALUATING SEED: When purchasing seeds, go for top-quality seeds from reputable dealers (many gardeners use the same seed company year after year). Seed sources that practice improper collecting, storing, or packaging practices may provide inferior seed. It might be old and out of date, for instance, or it may not grow to be true to the advertised name and claims. In rare cases, it might even carry diseases. One clue to a good quality supplier is that they guarantee their seeds in writing and offer fresh seed with high germination percentages, which will grow true.

GERMINATION PERCENTAGE: The percentage of live seeds capable of sprouting, or germination percentage, is generally stamped on the seed packet flap. The most reliable seeds will have over 90% germination, which means that 9 out of 10 seeds will sprout. When germination rates fall much below 80%, the results can be disappointing. There are a few exceptions. Alpine strawberries, chives, and watercress, as well as some heirlooms and rare plants, have lower germination rates—70% or even lower. If you plant extra seeds to make up for those that will not sprout, you can still get good value out of a packet of these seeds.

Many seed companies conduct their own germination tests before packaging and shipping out their seeds. You can do the same with homegrown or leftover seeds to determine the germination percentage.

SEEDS REQUIRING SCARIFICATION

These seeds have hard seed coats that need scarification—nicking the seed with a sharp knife or sanding the seed coat—to allow moisture to penetrate the seed and speed germination.

Camellia (*Camellia* spp.)
Cotoneaster (*Cotoneaster* spp.)
Flowering dogwood
     (*Cornus florida*)
Golden rain trees (*Koelreuteria* spp.)
Hawthorns (*Crataegus* spp.)
Hollies (*Ilex* spp.)
Honey locust (*Gleditsia* spp.)
Lotus (*Nelumbo* spp.)
Tree peony (*Paeonia potaninii*)
Wisterias (*Wisteria* spp.)

To test viability, moisten a double layer of paper towels. Spread 20 seeds on the towels and roll them up. Enclose the towel roll in a plastic bag and put it in a warm location. Check the paper-towel roll daily to make sure it is still moist and to see whether any seeds have germinated. Keep track of the number that have germinated successfully. If the germination rate is above 80%, the remainder of the packet is worth saving and sowing. If you have a limited number of seeds, the sprouted seeds could be plucked gently from the paper towels and planted in cell packs, pots, or flats of sterile peat-based seed-starting mix. If caught before they get too big and handled carefully, they may continue to grow.

FRESHNESS: The length of time seeds have been stored determines their freshness. As long as they are fully ripened and unencumbered by an after-ripening period, fresh seeds germinate best. Even some hard-to-germinate seeds such as angelica and Lenten roses will sprout immediately if they drop from the parent plant to the soil. But if collected and stored, they may remain dormant for a year or more. Many commercial seed houses stamp packages of fresh seeds with the current year and sell them before the next year. As summer arrives, seeds may be sold at deep discounts to clear out dated stock.

TRUENESS TO TYPE: Seedlings are often measured by the resemblance to the plants they claim to be. If hybrid plants are allowed to open-pollinate or if seeds are mixed up and packaged under the wrong name, they will not be true to type. Although this seldom happens to seed from a good-quality seed company, you should always be given a replacement packet or a full refund if seeds are not true to type.

When saving homegrown seed, special precautions may be necessary to ensure seeds will be true to type. This is especially important for crops that will cross-pollinate, or exchange pollen with other plants. A parent plant can be grown in isolation—a mile or more from others of its species or other related and interfertile plants, or it could be hand-pollinated.

When a flower first opens or is ready to open and before any bees or other pollinators visit it, it is suitable for hand-pollination. Use a clean, small paintbrush to collect pollen from the anthers of a suitable pollen donor plant. Remove any stamens from the newly opened flower and dab the collected pollen on the stigma. To be sure the pollination will work, you can repeat this process for the next several days. Keep the flower enclosed in a fine-mesh bag (this can be made from nylon hose) and secure the bag to the stem so that no pollen-carrying insects can make their way inside. Allow the seed pods or fruits to mature, then collect the ripe seeds. Gather seeds when dry pods begin to brown but before they split open. Seeds inside fleshy fruits (like tomatoes) are usually ready once the fruit is overripe.

SEED PACKETS: READ WITH CARE

Whether you purchase seeds off the rack or from a mail-order catalog, your most reliable source for specific information about when and how to start and grow seeds comes from the packet itself. Like a field guide, the seed packet points the way and offers sound advice to keep you from getting lost; paying attention to it lessens the chance of a serious misstep but doesn't guarantee success. Seed packets usually provide the basics: when to plant (outdoors or indoors), how long it takes the seeds to germinate, how far apart to space plants in the garden, and how long until the plant matures (flowers or fruits). Be sure to read carefully. For plants like tomatoes and peppers, seed packets indicate the number of days to maturity from the time of transplanting the seedling into the garden rather than from the sowing date. Because every garden is unique and nature unpredictable, days to maturity will vary from one garden to the next—and, remark-

ably, even from one year to another in the very same garden.

Instructions to sow the seeds outdoors indicate that the plant in question doesn't transplant well. Heed the advice and don't start the seeds indoors unless you grow them in a soil block, peat pellet, or peat pot, which can be planted directly into the garden without disturbing the roots when transplanting.

Some seed packets contain more information than others; they may even give suggestions on how to use the harvested plants. Still, few seed packets tell you in clear bold type whether the seeds inside are untreated, hybrid, or open-pollinated. For this reason, many gardeners prefer to order seeds from mail-order catalogs, establishing long-term relationships with a few suppliers whose seeds consistently deliver on their promise. Generally, seed companies respond to phoned-in questions and are more than pleased to make personal contact with their customers.

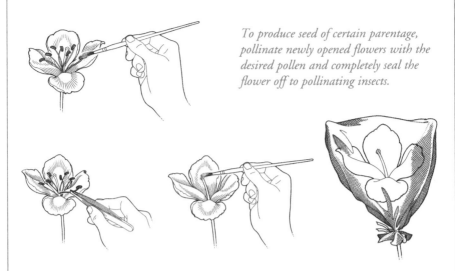

To produce seed of certain parentage, pollinate newly opened flowers with the desired pollen and completely seal the flower off to pollinating insects.

SEED SOURCES: Dozens of companies sell seeds through the mail. They advertise their offerings in catalogs ranging from glossy color magazines with hundreds of cultivars pictured and described to simple, single-page lists.

Mail-order shopping allows you to look for seeds and other supplies from the comfort of your home. This is particularly appealing because most catalogs arrive during winter when it is fun to think about gardening and plan the many things you want to grow. Catalogs can also provide a wide range of cultivars and species. Some specialize in seeds of vegetables, wildflowers, alpine plants, tropical exotics, herbs, perennials, or unusual annuals that might otherwise be hard to find.

You can also look for seeds on racks in garden centers, hardware stores, and even grocery stores. Seeds in racks tend to be less expensive than mail-order seeds but may not have all the high-performance characteristics that can be found in mail-order catalogs. The selection will also be smaller. But if you're a casual gardener or just looking to fill a gap after an early summer harvest, seed

OPEN-POLLINATED SEED SOURCES

A good reference book for avid gardeners looking for old-fashioned or open-pollinated vegetable cultivars is *Garden Seed Inventory*. This book, compiled by Seed Saver Publications, 3076 N. Winn Road, Decorah, IA 52101, has over 600 pages describing open-pollinated cultivars and listing their sources.

racks are convenient and worth frequenting for unexpected treasures.

Home gardeners can save seed from their own gardens. The easiest to keep true to name are plants such as lettuce, chicory, tomatoes, beans, and peas that self-pollinate, producing seed with their own pollen. To ensure purity, flowers should be bagged (detailed on page 41) to prevent accidental insect pollination.

Wildflowers and open-pollinated plants also are good for seed collecting and need not be specially managed for horticultural purity. Their natural variations are what make them so attractive. If you have wild woodland or prairie plants on your property, you could harvest a seed pod or two to grow more plants for your garden. But avoid harvesting seeds from wild plants in other natural areas, which could disrupt the species flow and ecology of the area.

Seed savers sometimes swap extra seeds for species they do not have. Some gardening magazines and plant societies organize lists of seeds available for swapping, some of which can be rare or unusual. But there may be little or no quality control so the seeds you receive may or may not be true, ripe, fresh, and viable. Still, the process is fun and you may make new friends.

HOW TO STORE LEFTOVER SEEDS

Most seed packets contain twice as much seed as you will use in a single planting. Why not save the rest for another time? A little special handling will help keep your seeds in good condition for a year or more.

Leave seeds in the original packet, if possible, to save the identification and planting information on the label. It should be completely dry. Simply fold over the open end of the packet, and seal it with tape.

Warm and moist conditions initiate germination, while cool and dry conditions postpone it—an important clue to how to store your seeds. Put several sealed seed packages in a canning jar with an airtight lid, and add a small envelope of dehydrated white rice or an antidesiccant such as silica gel to make sure the seeds stay dry in storage. Put the jar in a cool cupboard or in the basement until you need the seeds again.

SEED ACCESSORIES: Technological advances have made seed sowing convenient, and seeds easier to handle and plant. Here are some of the extra measures you might want to try.

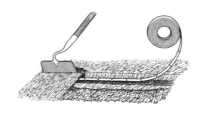

Seed tapes take the guesswork out of seed spacing in the garden.

SEED TAPES: Seeds of some annual flowers and vegetables are inserted at regular intervals into paper tapes, which can be unrolled and planted right in the garden. The paper tapes break down as the seeds grow without interfering with root development. There is no need to make individual planting holes or to calculate spacing. All that's required is to use a hoe to make a furrow of the proper depth in the garden. Stretch the tape along the bottom of the furrow and, with the hoe, refill the furrow to cover the tape with soil to the appropriate depth.

The selection of seeds available in tapes is limited and the cost is moderately high. Vegetable seed tapes are made primarily with fast-growing crops such as beets, carrots, dill, basil, lettuce, radishes, and spinach, all of which thrive when sown directly in the garden. There also are seed tapes of easily sown annual flowers such as cornflowers, cosmos, marigolds, and zinnias.

SEED PELLETS: It's easy to plant small seeds too thickly, encouraging disease and requiring thinning of the seedlings—pulling out weaker seedlings to provide growing room for the stronger ones. Very small seeds such as carrots may be coated with clay to turn them into larger pellets. Seed pellets make it possible to plant small seeds one by one, establishing ideal spacing right from the start. Once planted, the clay breaks down into the soil and the seed sprouts through it. Like seed tapes, however, pelleted seeds are more expensive—twice the price of unpelleted seeds—and available in a limited number of cultivars.

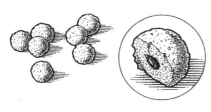

Seeds pelleted with clay are larger and easier to handle.

TREATED SEED: Some seeds, and corn in particular, may be treated with fungicides and should not be allowed in an organic garden. To avoid fungicide-treated

SEED-SAVING: A NATURAL ECONOMY

The seeds of many nonhybrid (open-pollinated) fruits, vegetables, and annuals can be saved, dried, stored, and germinated at home. Seed-saving harks back to the time when gardeners had to use every available local resource to regenerate their crop—most frequently, seeds started from their own plants in soil amended with homegrown decomposed vegetation (compost, although they didn't call it that back then).

There are practical benefits in saving seeds. Heirlooms can be shared with friends, often in exchange for other, hard-to-find varieties. The seeds germinated from homegrown plants in your organic garden will be free from synthetic chemicals.

Special care must be taken to preserve seed purity. Plants that can cross-pollinate with other species or varieties should be grown in isolation—a separate time or place from others. Self-pollinating crops such as peas and beans seldom need isolation.

The time to harvest flower or vegetable seeds approaches when the pods that contain them become dried out and appear ready to crack open, or when the fleshy vegetables or fruits containing them ripen fully on the vine (before rot can begin).

One way to harvest seeds from delicate pods is to secure a paper bag or piece of muslin over them before the pods split and the seeds scatter. When dried seeds are harvested, they can be scraped or shaken out of their pods onto newspaper and packaged.

The fleshy seeds found in melons, eggplant, tomatoes, cucumber, and members of the squash family present a different challenge. They must be separated out and washed thoroughly, then soaked for a few days in airtight, labeled glass containers filled with water until they sink and detach themselves from the surrounding pulp—which floats to the top and appears to ferment. Discard the (odoriferous) water through a mesh, and dry and keep the seeds.

Moisture is the seed-saver's adversary. To eliminate it, spread out all seeds—pod-dried and fleshy—to dry for a week or more, preferably on a screen in a non-windy place where air freely circulates. Don't pack the seeds until they have dried completely (the time will vary with the humidity).

To test whether seeds are live, a term called viable, you can conduct a sample germination test. Moisten a paper towel and sprinkle 5 or 10 seeds on it. Roll it up, place it in a plastic bag, and put in a warm place. If 8 out of 10 seeds sprout, the germination percentage is 80 percent, which is not bad. If it is lower than this, the seeds might produce scanty results.

seeds, buy from seed companies that sell only organically grown seed or at least offer untreated seed as an alternative to treated.

NITROGEN-FIXING BACTERIA FOR LEGUMES: A natural, beneficial bacteria, packaged in dark granules, can combine with legumes to help these plants fertilize themselves. As peas and beans emerge from their seeds and develop strong root systems, the nitrogen-fixing bacteria (primarily in the genus *Rhizobium*) penetrate the outer portion of the roots, forming small, round nodules. There they become half of a symbiotic, or mutually beneficial, partnership. The bacteria, nourished by the legume,

FINDING CHEMICAL-FREE SEEDS

Synthetic chemical fungicides, like Thiram and Captan, are commonly used by commercial seed producers to prevent diseases of seeds or seedlings, such as damping off. But when care is taken to handle seeds properly, fungicides are not necessary.

In an organic garden where soil is well drained and full of compost, disease organisms do not thrive. The same is true of peat-rich planting mixes, used to start seedlings indoors. As with outdoor gardens, containers used for indoor seed sowing must be able to drain freely so they won't become waterlogged.

It is also important to plant when soil temperatures are ideal for quick germination and growth of seeds— warm for heat-loving seeds and mild for cool-season seeds. Planting peas and lettuces too early, when the soil is cold and sodden, is a common mistake that invites disease problems.

Proper spacing, which is indicated on most seed packets, is another ticket to success with seeds. Giving each seed enough space to develop without crowding discourages damping off.

If you want to purchase chemical-free seeds, there is a wide range of sources. For example, you can seek out small, regional, mail-order catalogs that grow and sell chemically untreated, responsibly harvested seeds. These companies often carry an imaginative (if limited) selection of seeds suitable to the weather and soil conditions of your area. Specify "untreated seeds" when ordering from seed houses; most now stock them.

By using untreated seeds, you support companies concerned with the well-being of the environment; buying from a local organic grower supports environmentally conscious small businesses.

collect nitrogen from the air and fix it in a chemical form that plants can absorb and use like fertilizer. When the crop is through producing, cutting off and composting the old vines and leaving the nitrogen-rich nodules in the soil to decompose will provide nitrogen for whatever is planted there next.

Nitrogen-fixing bacteria can be used to coat the seeds of peas, beans, and other legumes before planting or can be sprinkled into the planting furrow before covering the seeds. Once an area has been treated with the bacteria granules, it will harbor the bacteria for years and benefit future crops.

There are special nitrogen-fixing bacteria inoculants formulated for peas and beans, fava beans and vetches, and soybeans. Be sure to buy a product that is appropriate for the legume you are planting. Other bacterial inoculants, which have nothing to do with nitrogen fixing and cannot be substituted for this purpose, encourage compost decomposition or improve the balance of beneficial microbes in the soil.

SEED-SOWING BASICS

Because all seeds need similar elements to germinate, the fundamentals of seed sowing apply to any seed, whether planted indoors or out.

TIMING SEED SOWING: The time of seed sowing is important because it determines whether seeds and seedlings will be set outdoors in mild, cool, or harsh weather. Cool-season crops grow well in cool and occasionally frosty weather. These plants can be sown directly outdoors when spring weather moderates or prestarted indoors in late winter or early spring to set out as seedlings in early to mid spring. (In warm southern states, they can be started in fall and grown as winter crops instead.)

Broccoli, if started from seed indoors and planted as 6-week-old seedlings outdoors, produces large heads ready for harvest in about 2 months. But if direct-sown outdoors, broccoli may take 3 or 4 months to be ready to harvest. Peas, which do not transplant well if prestarted indoors, should be planted directly outdoors just before the last frost date. They will be ready to pick in about 2 months.

VEGETABLES TO START INDOORS FROM SEED

Broccoli	Kale
Brussels sprouts	Kohlrabi
Cabbage	Lettuce
Cauliflower	Onion
Celery	Pepper
Collard	Tomato
Eggplant	

Cool-season vegetables and flowers can also be planted in summer for an autumn crop. Beets, broccoli, lettuce, and radishes are particularly mild and delicious when allowed to mature in cool, moist fall weather. Pansies and dianthus, summer-planted and sparkling with new blooms, are particularly enjoyable as the growing season wanes. Larkspurs, love-in-a-mist, pansies, snapdragons, and sweet alyssum are hardy enough in some climates to be sown in fall for an extra-early start in spring.

Other plants such as tomatoes are warm-season plants that will die if touched by frost or freezing temperatures. Their seed sowing needs to be timed so that they, or the seedlings that arise from them, will not be killed by cold. In Cleveland, Ohio, for example, the last spring frosts arrive in mid to late May. Tomato seed can be planted indoors from early to mid April, with the goal of setting out the seedlings 6 weeks later when the weather is reliably warm. Cucumbers, which also need frost-free weather, can be planted directly in the garden in late May or prestarted indoors 3 to 4 weeks earlier. As long as the soil is warm, both seeds and seedlings quickly grow into luxuriant vines.

Seedlings of hardy perennials often do best with a very early start— 10 weeks or more before spring temperatures become mild enough to plant. 'Snow Lady' shasta daisy, a charmer with clusters of 12"-high flowers through the summer, and 'Lavender Lady' lavender, with spikes of blue flowers in summer and fragrant silver foliage all year long, can bloom the first year if given a long head start indoors.

Timing also can be important with biennial plants such as cup-and-saucer plant, some foxgloves, and some hollyhocks. Biennials produce foliage the first year of growth and flowers the second year. To shorten this process, you can plant the seeds in early summer (perhaps after the spring pansies have finished blooming), fulfilling the foliage requirement during summer and fall and enjoying flowers the following year.

EASILY SOWN SEEDS: WARM- AND COOL-SEASON PLANTS

Most species produce seed suitable for sowing. Here are some of the easiest, listed by growing season.

WARM-SEASON ANNUAL FLOWERS

Canna (*Canna* spp.)
Cockscomb (*Celosia* spp.)
Geraniums (*Pelargonium* spp.)
Impatiens (*Impatiens* spp.)
Marigolds (*Tagetes* spp.)
Nasturtiums (*Nasturtium* spp.)
Petunias (*Petunia* spp.)
Salvias (*Salvia* spp.)
Sunflowers (*Helianthus annuus*)
Vinca (*Catharanthus roseus*)
Zinnias (*Zinnia* spp.)

WARM-SEASON ANNUAL VEGETABLES AND HERBS

Basil	Melons
Beans	Peppers
Corn	Potatoes
Cucumbers	Pumpkins
Dill	Squash
Eggplant	Summer
German	savory
chamomile	Tomatoes

COOL-SEASON FLOWERS

California poppy
  (*Eschscholzia californica*)
Dianthus (*Dianthus* spp.)
Flowering cabbage
  (*Brassica oleracea*)
Pansy (*Viola* × *wittrockiana*)
Pot marigold
  (*Calendula officinalis*)

Snapdragon (*Antirrhinum majus*)
Sweet pea (*Lathyrus odoratus*)

COOL-SEASON VEGETABLES AND HERBS

Arugula	Leeks
Beets	Lettuce
Broccoli	Onions
Cabbage	Parsley
Carrots	Parsnip
Cauliflower	Peas
Celery	Radishes
Cilantro	Radicchio
Kohlrabi	Turnips

PERENNIAL HERBS

Chives	Oregano
Fennel	Sage
Lovage	Sorrel

PERENNIAL FLOWERS

Columbine (*Aquilegia* spp.)
Coreopsis (*Coreopsis grandiflora*
  'Early Sunrise')
Mountain bluet
  (*Centaurea montana*)
Orange coneflower
  (*Rudbeckia fulgida*)
Purple coneflower
  (*Echinacea purpurea*)
Shasta daisy (*Leucanthemum
  maximum* 'Snow Lady')
Viola (*Viola cornuta*)

SOWING SEEDS: Regardless of whether you are starting seeds indoors or directly in the garden, the most important aspect to sowing is planting seeds at the right depth, usually indicated on the seed packet. In general, smaller seeds are planted shallowly, while larger seeds more deeply. For very small seeds such as begonias and petunias—which are the size of poppy seeds or smaller—sprinkling them on the surface of the growing mix and tapping the mix down with your fingers is enough coverage. For medium-size seeds such as broccoli and cauliflower—which are about the size of sesame seeds—a ¼"-deep hole or furrow will suffice. Large seeds such as beans, peas, or cannas need a hole about 1" deep.

Individual seeds can go in shallow holes in single or double rows.

When planting, you can use several techiques to set the seeds in the soil or mix. The most precise method is to make a hole for each seed using a pencil, stick, or your finger. Insert the seed, then press the soil or mix back to refill the hole. A faster but less controlled method is to make a planting furrow with a pencil or straight edge indoors or a hoe outdoors. Carefully drop the seeds at the proper spacing (the seed packet will advise) along the length of the furrow, then cover them. You can also broadcast the seed, sprinkling it sparingly over the soil or growing mix, and layering more soil or mix over the top to achieve the proper depth. This method, although fast, easy, and good for small plants, usually requires some thinning of overcrowded seedlings.

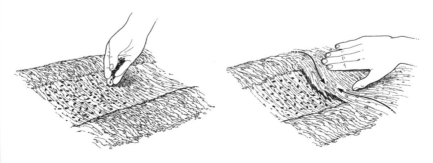

For a big yield of leafy vegetables, broadcast the seeds over a wide bed.

YOUNG SEEDLING CARE:

Seedlings require slightly different care than mature plants—more attention to watering, gentle fertilizing at special times, appropriate quantities of light, and precautions to prevent diseases.

Seedlings, like seeds, need to be kept evenly moist throughout their early life. Their small roots are confined near the surface of the soil and if that dries out, the seedlings will die. Water frequently and shallowly at first; wait until the seedlings become large with deep, well-established roots to drench the soil deeply and infrequently. Watering methods will vary depending on whether seedlings are indoors or outside (see page 21).

Young seedlings grown indoors require a steady diet of light. While seedlings will grow with 12 hours of light a day, it's best to provide 14 to 16 hours of light per day when they are in early stages of development. A fluorescent light garden operated by an automatic timer is the seed-starter's best friend to insure a consistent schedule of light for seedlings.

Even when they are grown in nutrient-free, peat-based mixes, seeds and new seedlings need no fertilizer; they are nourished by endosperm stored within the seed. Most commercial peat-based seed-starting mixes and live-soil mixes enriched by compost, contain a small amount of fertilizer that will take over providing nutrients where the seed leaves off. For most seedlings grown indoors—where light levels are never as intense as outdoors—this is enough fertilizer to support seedlings through 6 weeks of growth.

SOWING SMALL SEEDS IN A FLAT

To make small seeds easier to handle, mix them with an equal amount of builder's sand (available from a hardware store or garden center) in a salt shaker and broadcast by lightly shaking over the flat. Don't use beach sand unless it's been thoroughly rinsed. The salt shaker method produces fairly even spacing so that thinning is kept to a minimum. Another method is to sow directly from the seed packet by pinching its sides together, creating a funnel down the center of one flap. (This seems to allow more control than sowing seeds out of the side of the top.) Or, you can take small seeds between your thumb and forefinger and, with a rotating motion, drop them into the rows of the flat.

There are occasional exceptions. Fertilizer may be needed if seedlings are grown outdoors or in bright greenhouses in peat-based mixes, or if they stay in the same container for more than 6 weeks. In these cases, you should apply a balanced fertilizer, one which has similar percentages of nitrogen, phosphorus, and potassium. The percentages of each of these major nutrients are noted on fertilizer package labels. On organic fertilizers, they could range from 2-2-2 to 5-5-5 or various combinations within that range, all of which are acceptable. Water the seedlings with a half-strength solution of water-soluble fertilizer every couple of weeks, or apply a slow-release, granular, organic fertilizer every month to 6 weeks. Be careful not to apply too much, especially high nitrogen fertilizers (with a ratio such as 5-1-1). This may force fast growth at the expense of a strong and sturdy constitution.

Seeds planted outdoors in organic-rich soil may have all the nutrients they need to produce an entire crop—especially if, like legumes, they can fix their own nitrogen. But heavy-feeding seedlings of plants such as cabbage and tomatoes will grow faster with an extra dose of fertilizer once they have at least two sets of leaves and are growing strongly.

Seedlings, which are tender when they sprout, are susceptible to a variety of soil-borne diseases such as root rot, which kills seedling roots, and damping off, a fungus that eats through the base of the seedling stem. These can be avoided by careful growing practices. Avoid over-watering, as soggy soil eliminates air and encourages diseases; plant in a well-drained growing medium, ideally in peat-based growing mixes that are sterile and have natural antifungal properties; and sow seeds sparingly instead of in thick clumps, so each seedling has open space around it and fresh air circulation. Thin out, by pulling or cutting out weaker seedlings, if seedlings arise in bunches.

Thin out overcrowded seedlings so the remainder can thrive. Edible thinnings can go in the salad bowl.

TRANSPLANTING TIME: The ideal time for transplanting seedlings, whether started indoors or out, is when they have two sets of true leaves—above and beyond their seed cotyledons. Make sure their roots have grown strong

PREVENTING PEST DAMAGE TO YOUNG TRANSPLANTS

Fresh, young transplants may need extra protection against a whole host of garden pests. A simple paper or metal collar around a plant will thwart slugs, snails, and cutworms. A paper cup or tuna can is perfect—just remove the bottom of the cup or can and slip it over the new transplant in the garden. Be sure that at least 1" of the collar is below soil level, with the rest sticking above the soil. Ideally, there should be no more than an inch of space between the collar and the stem of the plant.

Another way to discourage slugs and snails is to make a circle about 1" wide and ¼"–½" high around the plant with diatomaceous earth (available inexpensively and in large quantity at pool supply stores, more costly at garden centers). It abrades the soft bellies of these creatures when they crawl across it, drawing moisture and desiccating them.

Some birds and rabbits find young plants irresistible. New transplants can easily be protected with a loose covering of chicken wire or bird netting. Form several hoops from wire hangers and slip the chicken wire or netting over them. Be sure the covering goes all the way to the ground—some critters can be persistent!

Be sure at least 1" of the protective collar is below soil level. A paper collar takes little time to biodegrade; tin can be removed after 3–4 weeks (if it threatens to damage the plant) or left in the ground and covered with mulch.

enough to support the seedling when transplanted, but are still small and straight enough that they are not tangled or matted. The method used for transplanting will vary depending on where the seedling is grown. (See pages 55 and 56.)

OUTDOOR AFTER-CARE: Seedlings growing outdoors need to be planted in ideal conditions—full sun or shade, rich or lean soil. Plant preferences vary with species and even with cultivars, so read seed packets, seed catalogs, and gardening books to identify what is best for each plant you grow. This practice is especially important for young seedlings as they are at a weak stage of development.

DAMPING OFF

Damping off is a fungal disease that can kill off seedlings in a single day. If your seedlings are wilted and there is a dark and rotten area at the base of the stem at the soil line, remove the diseased seedlings at once and destroy them. Inspect neighboring seedlings growing in the same container and remove them at the first sign of disease. Cut back on watering, and make sure the seedlings are getting enough light and air circulation.

There is one common thread to all seedlings. Until they become well established, they require moist soil. Water as needed and mulch, if desired, to prevent the soil surface from drying out. If, despite this attention, newly planted seedlings wilt, you can shade them for a week or two by setting an upright board to the south- or west-facing side, partially blocking the sun until the roots are strong enough to support the plant.

Annual flowers, such as browallia, and perennials like asters and chrysanthemums should be pinched to encourage branching. When seedlings are 4"–6" high, pinch off the tip of the stem with your fingernails or pruning shears, and repeat this process several times until early summer, particularly with asters and chrysanthemums. This will result in a handsome, bushy plant. But you should avoid pinching later in summer or you risk removing flower buds that you'll want to enjoy in fall.

PRESTARTING SEEDLINGS INDOORS

Indoor seed sowing requires a specific routine to ensure that seeds get everything they need. But once you learn the routine, the process is easy and effective.

Begin by calculating the proper timing. Check the sowing information on the seed packets and on page 47 to help determine when to start your seeds. If you plant in flats, you'll be able to raise a large quantity of seeds in a small area, but you will have to move the seedlings to individual containers later. If you plant your seeds in individual containers or cell packs, you will not have to transplant seedlings into larger containers.

Begin with a peat-based seed-starting mix and plant at a proper depth and spacing. Cover the planting container with clear plastic wrap and set it in a warm place so the seeds can germinate. Check them every day— some seeds can sprout in as little as 3 days and need to be put into bright light right away. If sunlight is unreliable, put the seedlings under fluorescent lights with a timer set to turn them on for 14 to 16 hours a day.

Water indoor pots, flats, cell packs, soil blocks, and plug trays as often as necessary to keep the seed-starting mix moist. You can drizzle water gently from overhead or set pots briefly in a container of lukewarm water to let them soak water up from below. Smaller pots or flats may need daily watering, especially during hot weather. Larger and deeper pots will hold more moisture and dry out at a slightly slower rate.

POTTING ON: Seedlings grown in flats or trays will soon need more space than a flat can supply to accommodate a growing root system and allow free foliage growth. For example, tomatoes started indoors in plug trays or flats may be spaced a ½″ apart. But for them to grow, flower, and fruit, each plant needs a square of growing space at least 18″ wide. This calls for transplanting into more spacious accommodations.

TRANSPLANTING FROM FLATS: Slip one hand under the growing mix and uproot a clump of seedlings, keeping the roots together in the

While it's usual to transplant seedlings when they have two sets of leaves, it can be done earlier.

mix. Gently grasp the base of one stem and tease it apart from the others, using care to keep the ball of roots intact. If any roots have become matted or overgrown, untangle them carefully.

Once a seedling is uprooted and separated, replant it immediately in a separate cell pack, or a 3", 4", or 6" pot—the size will vary depending on how long you intend to keep the seedling in that particular container. Fill the container with moist peat-based planting mix and make a hole in the center deep enough to accommodate the roots without twisting or knotting them at the base.

Lower the roots into the hole, setting the seedling at the same depth it was growing at previously. (Tomatoes and other seedlings that arise with a single stem, however, are an exception to this rule. If they have become lanky from growing in less than ideal light indoors, you can cover the stem base with soil. This provides extra support and can encourage more root growth from the covered stem.) Firm the soil lightly around the roots and keep the mix moist, which will be especially important while the roots recover from their transplantation.

Soil blocks are equally easy to transplant. When roots penetrate through the cube, scoop up the cube in your fingers and set it in an appropriate-size depression in a larger soil block or a pot of live soil mix somewhat larger than the cube.

Hardening Off: Seedlings grown indoors or in a greenhouse will need to be hardened off—toughening their tissues in preparation for the bright sun, strong winds, and pounding rain they will meet outdoors— before they will be ready for transplanting into the garden. This step can be the most important in the seed-starting process as seedlings are more susceptible to the whims of nature than hardier specimens.

To harden off seedlings, or toughen them up for outdoor growing, they require a period of gradual acclimation to the outdoors. Start by setting seedlings outside in a shady location for several hours a day. When set outside in containers, seedlings also are prone to wilting, so be sure to keep the soil moist. Over the next week, gradually increase exposure to sunlight and wind, bringing seedlings indoors for a recovery break if they wilt or suffer from sunscald, indicated by burnt yellow patches on the foliage from unaccustomed sun exposure. After about a week without setbacks, the seedlings will be sturdy enough to transplant into the garden.

PLANTS TO START IN SOIL BLOCKS OR PEAT PELLETS INDOORS OR DIRECT-SEED IN THE GARDEN

These plants will do well when transplanted in soil blocks or peat pellets to keep their roots intact. Quick-growers can also be direct sown (see page 58).

Ageratum
   (*Conoclinium coelestinum*)
Beet (*Beta vulgaris*)
Begonias (*Begonia* spp.)
Calendulas (*Calendula* spp.)
Carrot (*Daucus carota*)
Cosmos (*Cosmos* spp.)
Cucumber (*Cucumis sativus*)
Flowering tobaccos (*Nicotiana* spp.)
Four o'clock (*Mirabilis jaropa*)
Geranium
   (*Pelargonium* × *hortorum*)
Impatiens (*Impatiens* spp.)
Lobelias (*Lobelia* spp.)
Marigolds (*Tagetes* spp.)

Petunias (*Petunia* spp.)
Phlox (*Phlox* spp.)
Pumpkins (*Cucurbita* spp.)
Salvias (*Salvia* spp.)
Snapdragons (*Antirrhinum* spp.)
Spiderflowers
   (*Cleome hassleriana; Grevillea* spp.)
Squashes summer and winter
   (*Cucurbita* spp.)
Sweet alyssum
   (*Lobularia maritima*)
Swiss chard (*Beta vulgaris* var.
   flavescens)
Turnip (*Brassica rapa*)
Verbenas (*Verbena* spp.)

TRANSPLANTING OUTDOORS: Evaluate the seedling carefully before transplanting it outdoors so you're sure to handle it in the best possible manner. Lanky seedlings with long, barren stem bases can be set in the ground slightly deep, providing extra support for a stronger start. Roots that have become root-bound, solidly packed inside a small container, should be loosened up so they are free to grow into the surrounding soil. You can use a sharp knife to break up any solid masses of roots. If the roots are only tangled, work them free with your fingers, taking care not to break them.

Starting with well-prepared soil, make a hole deep enough to hold the roots (and the bottom of the stem if necessary). Fill the hole with a half-strength, water-soluble fertilizer such as fish emulsion, which will provide enough nutrients to get the seedling off to a strong start. Set the seedling into the hole, spreading out the roots so that they can grow in different directions, and refill the hole with good soil. Keep the seedlings moist until they are well established. Mulching around the planting site will help prevent the soil from drying out and will discourage weeds, which compete with the seedling for sun, moisture, and nutrients.

Direct-Sown Seeds Outdoors

When sowing seeds directly outdoors, soil management, spacing, and the method of sowing become considerations. Plant seeds in well-worked, finely pulverized soil. Make sure the soil doesn't crust over, or form a hard surface layer after being pounded with rain or sprinklers. Crusted soil can have low oxygen levels and can physically prevent delicate seeds such as carrots from arising. Crusting can be minimized if you cover the seeds with fine compost or coarse sand instead of silt or clay soil. You can also interplant vigorous growing radish seeds with carrot and other delicate seeds. The radishes arise first, breaking up compacted soil and making way for the easy emergence of carrot seeds. It also helps

---

DIRECT SEED IN THE GARDEN

These flowers and vegetables may not transplant well and can be seeded directly in the garden.

Baby's breath
  (*Gypsophila paniculata*)
Bachelor's button
  (*Centaurea cyanus*)
Bean (*Phaseolus vulgaris*)
Beet (*Beta vulgaris*)
Butterfly weed
  (*Aesclepius tuberosum*)
Calendula (*Calendula officinalis*)
Carrot (*Daucus carota*)
Corn (*Zea mays*)
Cosmos (*Cosmos* spp.)
Cucumber (*Cucumbis sativus*)
Flossflower (*Ageratum housitanum*)

Flowering tobaccos
  (*Nicotiana* spp.)
Four o'clocks (*Mirabilis jalapa*)
Larkspur (*Consolida ambigua*)
Love-in-a-mist (*Nigella* spp.)
Nasturtium
  (*Tropaeolum majus*)
Okra (*Abelmoschus esculentus*)
Pea (*Pisum sativum*)
Spiderflower (*Cleome hasslerana*)
Stock (*Matthiola incana*)
Sweet pea (*Lathyrus odoratus*)
Turnip (*Brassica rapa*)
Verbenas (*Verbena* spp.)

if you keep the seed beds moist by watering with drip or trickle irrigation systems that gently ooze water at soil level.

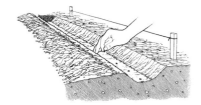

You have to decide whether to set seeds in rows or broadcast them across wide beds. If you plant seeds

Space seeds precisely in a furrow, which is easily made with the corner of a hoe.

in individual rows, a method that works well with corn, you will have space to walk or cultivate between rows, but you will have wasted much good growing room. To make sure your planting rows are straight, run a string between two stakes set at either end of the desired planting area. Make a furrow below the string with your hoe. The furrow should be the ideal depth for the seed, as indicated on the seed packet. Remove the string and drop the seeds one by one into the furrow at the recommended spacing. If you are planting seeds with a low germination percentage, you can space them more thickly than recommended. Use the hoe to cover the seeds with soil to the surrounding level, and label the end of the row with the cultivar name.

Sowing seeds in wide beds—2'–3' across—allows more concentrated planting of small crops such as lettuces, carrots, radishes, or beans, and keeps feet off to the side so they do not compress good growing soil. Rake the garden soil into a low mound about 6" high and 2'–3' across. The area beside the bed will be lower and serve as a footpath. Use a hoe to flatten the surface of the wide bed and then scrape off the top several inches of soil. Keep the extra soil in ridges at the edges of the wide beds.

Take a handful of seeds and squeeze them out one by one between your finger and thumb to sprinkle them sparingly across the wide bed. Rake back the soil ridges from the perimeter of the bed with your hoe to cover the seeds. Label the planting area with the cultivar name.

When finished sowing in a wide bed, gently cover seeds with extra soil from the sidelines.

If you want to transplant seedlings that have been started outdoors, slip a hand trowel deep under a seedling that has at least two true leaves and lever it up with a clump of soil-encased roots. Put the seedling in a flat or another container that will protect the root ball from shifting around and breaking up. Transport the seedling to its new location and transplant it right away, before the roots dry out. Set the seedling at the same depth in the soil as it was originally growing. Keep it moist until growing strongly. This is also a great way to use self-sown seedlings of flowers such as Johnny-jump-up, calendula, and snapdragons.

STEM CUTTINGS

Stem cuttings are sections of young stems that, when severed from their parent plant, will root and grow into perfect replicas of the original. And they have many distinct advantages over other methods of propagation. Stems of plants such as geraniums, dahlias, mints, and watercress root quickly. With just a few weeks of care, these cuttings will be ready to go out into the garden and perform as well as their parent plants. This is fast work compared to seedlings.

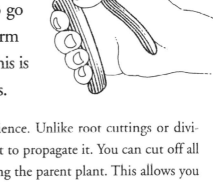

Stem cuttings also offer convenience. Unlike root cuttings or division, you don't need to dig up a plant to propagate it. You can cut off all the stems you need without disrupting the parent plant. This allows you to propagate trees and shrubs, including roses, that won't tolerate repeated root disturbance. It also lets you grow a unique plant from a friend's garden without a lot of bother.

Herbaceous, softwood, and hardwood stems have the ability to root, although some are quicker than others. Their age and firmness will determine how you should handle them.

HERBACEOUS CUTTINGS: The easiest cuttings are herbaceous cuttings, made from the soft stems of nonwoody plants such as begonias, impatiens, coleus, basil, chrysanthemums, wisteria, and other annual and perennial flowers and herbs. They are quick to resprout roots, which can be particularly satisfying.

There is a clear economic advantage to these cuttings. One great plant can become many. For instance, a gallon pot of plumbago (*Ceratostigma plumbaginoides*), a creeping ground cover bearing crystal blue flowers in late summer and fall and carpets of red leaves in autumn, could be multiplied into five, ten, or more new plants. Cuttings started in spring will be ready to plant in early summer and well established by fall.

You can root cuttings of tender plants (those that die when nipped by frost and winter cold) in late summer or fall to keep indoors during

CUTTING CAUTIONS

Plants grown from cuttings are only as good as the parent plant they come from. That's why you should avoid taking cuttings of diseased plants, which contaminate their offspring and, possibly, other plants around them. If, for instance, your tomato plants are drooping, dying, and stricken with wilt, attempting to save the crop by clipping off the still green tip of a stem to root would do you no good. The wilt disease will continue to work on the cutting, making it flat and lifeless in little time.

Many commercial propagators test their parent plants for diseases before using them for propagation. In a process called indexing, they can identify the presence of viruses and other diseases, weeding out unhealthy specimens. Even though amateur propagators don't bother indexing, you can buy certified, disease-free plants (which come from indexed parents) and take cuttings from them. Or at the least, choose cuttings from vigorous, healthy parent plants that show no stunting, contorting, unusual dwarfing, discoloration, or other problems indicative of diseases.

Most but not every plant grown from stem cuttings comes true, or resembles its parent exactly. One exception is variegated plants, with foliage marked silver or gold. If started from stem cuttings, variegated plants often become plain green. This is because the genetic origin of variegation usually springs from cells located elsewhere in the plant, not on the stem.

Plants that are patented are protected from propagation, even by you. For a period of 20 years, the plant breeder or discoverer can control who grows the plant. Usually commercial propagators are licensed by the patentor and pay a royalty for the rights to propagate a patented plant.

winter. Try this with a rose-scented geranium to enjoy the lovely perfume all winter long, or use the leaves to flavor cakes and cookies with soft aroma. In early spring, the wintered plants will provide enough stem cuttings for a whole bed of rose-scented geraniums.

SOFTWOOD CUTTINGS:

These are made from young stems of woody plants, which will root but not always as quickly as herbaceous cuttings. There is no perfect texture for a softwood cutting but you can use new stems that range from soft to slightly firm.

For several weeks after new tree and shrub stems emerge, they are succulent and soft, tender enough that you can pinch them

For softwood cuttings, select new growth that has reached the correct firmness.

off with your fingernails. For a few plants, including lilacs, these baby-fresh new shoots are prime for rooting. They will need special attention—high humidity and moderate to bright light—to keep them plump, vigorous, and intent on rooting.

Many other trees and shrubs, however, will root more reliably if your cuttings are taken from firmer shoots, new growth that has begun to mature as spring turns to summer. Ideal stems are firm enough to snap like a garden-fresh green bean when bent in two. This condition often exists about the time when light green spring leaves darken into summer emerald and when the spring garden is completely planted. If spring arrives early, however, and hot weather follows quickly, new shoots will firm up faster. Plan to take the cuttings earlier when they are in perfect condition.

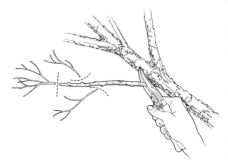

HARDWOOD CUTTINGS:

Woody stems that are a year old and fully firm are ripe for this kind

Hardwood cuttings come from dormant, year-old stems.

of propagation. Taken in late fall after the leaves drop, hardwood cuttings are handled differently from herbaceous and softwood cuttings. They spend the winter dormant, then awaken in early spring to sprout roots before the leaf buds swell and open.

Fewer hardwood cuttings may root than softwood cuttings. Forsythias, for example, will start from softwood and hardwood cuttings. If you make a dozen of each you may end up with six rooted hardwood cuttings and ten rooted softwood cuttings. Hardwood cuttings are extra-easy to make and plant so you can start extra to allow for some failures. They need a cold period of dormancy until early spring, when they can be planted outdoors in a cold frame or sheltered nursery bed.

STRUCTURE OF A STEM

Botany, although not everyone's favorite college subject, may gain new respect among gardeners. Knowing stem parts and how they affect the stem cutting becomes of real-life importance to a propagator—not just a study in memorization. Exploring stems and noting the similarities and differences between species and seasons makes a gardener a keen judge of plants. Observing the way the foliage is arranged on the stem, where the small dormant buds lie in wait for a chance to sprout, and how firm or woody the tissue is will make you a more proficient propagator. Here are some of the stem parts vital for stem cuttings.

Bark is the smooth or corky tissue forming an external skin on woody plants. It protects stems from pathogens and from drying out. The interior layer of bark is vascular tissue called phloem, which transports food photosynthesized in the foliage to other parts of the plant, including the roots. If the bark is severed around the entire width of a stem, food, which can no longer travel down through the interrupted phloem, will accumulate just above where the bark was cut, encouraging root development.

The *cambium layer* is a layer of unspecialized cells (like a blank canvas) that lies in the wood just beneath the bark of many trees and shrubs. Cambium cells have full memory of the genetic codes needed to create any part of a plant and can regenerate into new roots on stem cuttings or new shoots on root cuttings.

Buds are plant embryos, complete with shoots, leaves, or flowers, often enclosed in protective scales. They are able to lie dormant until stimulated into growth. How quickly growth buds break dormancy depends largely on their position, and hence priority, on the plant.

Terminal buds sit at the tip of a branch or shoot and are the first to open and begin growing in spring. Magnolias have particularly handsome terminal buds that are large and covered with furry scales. Terminal buds produce growth hormones called auxins that cause rapid shoot elongation and prevent axillary buds lower on the branch from sprouting.

Axillary buds lie lower on the stem, in the node or junction where the leaf attaches to the stem. On a foliated stem, these lie dormant unless needed rather like insurance. If gypsy moths consume all the leaves on a branch or a gardener pinches the lower leaves off a stem cutting, axillary buds will replace the missing growth. Axillary buds will sprout into new side shoots if the terminal bud with its hormonal dominance is removed, which is why pinching annual flowers makes them bushy.

Adventitious buds arise in other places—often as a response to wounding. In the case of stem cuttings, adventitious buds may grow into roots near the lower cut on the stem, allowing severed stems to resume all the functions of ordinary plants.

Flower buds may be located near the terminal bud or amid axillary buds. They may be fatter than vegetative or growth buds, often plump, frequently assuming the color of the flower before opening. Flower buds have no place on stem cuttings. If allowed to remain on a cutting, they will sap energy from the stem and limit rooting.

Nodes, like the intersections of two busy streets, are places on the stem where leaves and side shoots emerge from a mother branch. On sugar maples, nodes are slightly enlarged and marked with a crescent of darker bark. Nodes also harbor axillary buds, found at the base of leaves.

An *internode* is the expanse of stem that lies between two nodes. The length of an internode indicates how fast a plant has been growing and determines how long your cuttings should be. Slower-growing stems have shorter internodes and a greater concentration of leaves and buds in a smaller area. Often, they can be much easier to work with than stems with long internodes.

TIPS AND TECHNOLOGY

Having the right equipment on hand before you begin taking cuttings will help the process go smoothly.

KEEPING RECORDS: A record of your successes and failures is an invaluable aid for future projects, as you learn to size up different kinds of stems and to provide ideal growing conditions for them according to their maturity, length, and species. Note the date you took the cuttings; the condition of the stems; the length of the cuttings you made; the type of hormone treatments you used, if any; the kind of growing medium used; the light and humidity levels; and the speed and reliability of rooting. Once you have made these initial notations, in the future you need only note dates, changes made to the procedure, and whether the results were improved.

For an easy and informal record-keeping system, a daily planner will allow you to jot down what you've seen and done day by day. Keep the planner on your desk, in your garden room, or in some other convenient place where you will be reminded to update it.

A more organized approach is an index-card file. Each card can focus on a single species or a single cultivar. For instance, you can compare the differences between rooting stem cuttings of full-size 'Gray Lady' lavender with dwarf 'Munstead' lavender. The time spent on developing an index-card file is repaid in easy reference on a later date.

Computerized record-keeping systems provide yet another alternative. Look for record-keeping garden software or make your own. It's easy to establish a format for storing the information you need and compiling it electronically in a report, a graph, or a critical analysis.

CUTTING TOOLS: When taking cuttings, use a sharp knife or scissors-type pruning shears that will cut cleanly through the stem without mashing it. If you feel resistance when slicing through a stalk of celery, rhubarb, or a flowering twig, get out a knife sharpener and hone the blade well.

Be prepared to sterilize your pruning shears or knife before you take cuttings from different plants so you won't spread diseases from one to the other with infected tools. This is particularly important when working with disease-prone plants such as fruit trees. To sterilize pruning equipment, rub your knife or shears with a rag dampened with a solution of 1 part bleach in 10 parts water, or dip them in Lysol disinfectant or isopropyl alcohol, which are efficient

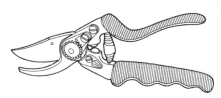

Bypass pruning shears

Propagating knife

and less likely to corrode blades than bleach. When finished for the day, rinsing the blades and drying them well will help keep them from rusting.

ROOTING HORMONES: Although plants do not have neurological systems like animals, they can still transmit messages from one part of the plant to another. They do this with hormones, chemicals that elicit varying effects on the tissues with which they interact. Hormones in a class called auxins are responsible for initiating rooting in stem cuttings but must be present immediately after the cutting is made. Ancient European farmers slipped a seed of grain into the base of a new cutting to encourage rooting, knowing it helped but not knowing why. Grain seeds exude auxins.

Softwood tip cuttings or herbaceous cuttings may produce all the rooting hormone they need naturally because their terminal buds manufacture auxins. But cuttings that are dormant (such as hardwood cuttings, see page 78) or without terminal buds will root more reliably if you give them an extra dose of rooting hormones immediately after making the cutting.

A grain seed is no longer necessary because rooting hormones are available in many garden centers or garden supply catalogs. There are several brands available, each containing different concentrations and blends of natural and synthetic hormones plus some extras. One superior product contains auxins and the nutrient boron, which encourages rooting naturally. Some rooting hormones, most notably popular Rootone, may include a fungicide that is unacceptable in organic gardens. If you are planning to take a large number of cuttings, consider using a liquid rooting hormone. It tends to penetrate stems much more evenly than powders.

Apply rooting hormones to fresh cut stems according to the package directions with these added cautions. Don't dip the cut stems into the original container of hormone; they could spread contaminants. Instead, pour powdered rooting hormones into a corner of a clean paper envelope or make a small pile on a paper towel and dip the stems in the powder. Shake any excess powder off the cuttings or it could retard rooting. The old saying, if a little is good, a lot is better, definitely does not apply here. Seal the original jar to keep the powder clean and free from moisture. If you store it in the refrigerator, it will keep fresh up to a year.

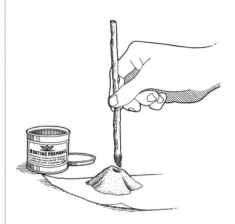

Rooting hormones, applied to freshly cut stems, encourage good results from hard-to-root species.

When using liquid formulations, pour 1" (if not otherwise specified on the label) of the liquid into a clean cup. You can use a narrow jigger to dip stems one by one or a broad-bottom dish to dip a bundle of stems at the same time. Seal and store the original container, but don't be surprised if the liquid hormones lose their effectiveness more quickly than powdered hormones do.

ROOTING MEDIA AND CONTAINERS: Just as garden soil must be tilled and amended before adding a single seed, the rooting medium for cuttings must be prepared, moistened, and set in a container, ready to go as soon as the cuttings are prepared. Cuttings need a moist but well-drained, airy, and sterile rooting medium (see page 17 for more details). You can use a variety of different substances for stem cuttings, none of which are actual soil, hence the name rooting medium rather than potting soil. A classic blend is equal parts peat moss and perlite or coarse sand.

Plants with succulent stems like cacti, furry or silver leaves like lamb's ears, or needlelike or leathery leaves like rosemary are adapted for dry conditions. To prevent them from rotting, provide a well-drained growing mix of perlite or coarse sand alone.

Wet the rooting medium thoroughly until it feels like a moist sponge and put a layer several inches deep in a container. Deeper layers accommodate longer cuttings and provide extra rooting space that can make transplanting easier.

You can put rooting medium in a variety of different containers. Flats, pots, clear plastic boxes, or even a glass aquarium will work as long as the container has holes in the bottom for water drainage. If you are using a recycled container, scrub it out well, then sterilize it with a solution of 1 part bleach in 9 parts water. For softwood or herbaceous cuttings, plan to cover the container with a clear top or plastic tent to create a humid, greenhouselike environment. (For details on tenting, see page 10).

Long nursery flats are best if you're making dozens of similar cuttings that root at the same rate. But cuttings of a variety of different species can be managed more efficiently when rooted in separate containers or separated in divided flats so faster rooters can be removed without disturbing slower rooters. Reluctant rooters are best mass planted in individual pots so unproductive cuttings won't waste space.

To save time, put easily rooted cuttings in cell packs. (If appropriate, recycle the cell packs you bought with your spring annual flowers.) Well-rooted cuttings grown in cell packs can go right out in the garden without repotting, but careful attention to watering is required to get to that point. Each individual cell must be moistened—and never missed—when the pack is watered or they will quickly dry out.

CUTTING BASICS

Some of the same principles and practices apply to any type of stem cutting. These are the basics, which like preparing a rich soil bed, provide a strong foundation for you to grow proficient as a propagator.

TAKING CUTTINGS: The procedure of removing stems from the parent plant in preparation for propagating them as cuttings is the first step in the propagating process. Similar to sowing fresh, highly viable seeds, you need stems that are in top condition to make the propagation effort worthwhile.

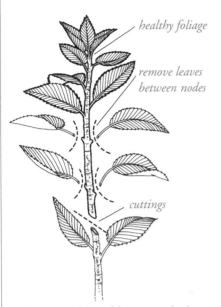

healthy foliage

remove leaves
between nodes

cuttings

Removing lower foliage, or side shoots,
provides an open expanse of stem to
submerge for rooting.

Good health—reflected in bright green leaves, solid stems, and regular growth—is essential. Stems burgeoning with flowers, fruit, or seeds—all of which drain energy from the stem—are less desirable but may be salvaged if you remove the flowers, fruit, or seeds.

You can use the plant's natural biorhythms to garner even better cutting material by taking cuttings in the morning, when the stems are full of moisture after a cool, moist evening. (Morning is also a great time to harvest herbs, lettuces, and other leafy vegetables.) If you are working during a drought, water the parent plant well the night before taking cuttings to prevent moisture stress. Since cuttings may be without active roots for at least several weeks, starting with a full tank of water can be the key to success.

MAKING CUTTINGS: Not to be confused with *taking* cuttings, making cuttings describes the process of sectioning a stem into individual pieces. At the bare minimum, cuttings need 2 nodes or sets of leaves each. Making them this small will give you the maximum number of new starts from a limited number of parent stems. If parent material is not at a minimum, you can make longer cuttings, with 4, 6, or more nodes. Longer stems have more stored food and photosynthesizing foliage to support root growth, but they also lose more moisture through the foliage. Most cuttings will end up between 1"–6" long.

Sever the cutting at a 45° angle slightly below a bud or node. Angling the lower cut on any cutting is a good habit to get into. Although it provides more surface area beneath which rooting will occur, it is not essential to the overall success of your rooting. What it does is clearly indicate which part of the cutting is the lower end, the end that must always be planted in the soil. You'll appreciate this tip most when making hard-

THE MASTER PROPAGATOR

Just as feeling the loose, spongy tilth of a dark, organic-rich soil lets a master gardener know the bed is ready for fabulous potatoes or phlox, learning differences in stem conditions tells a master propagator when a stem is ready to root. Here are some examples.

BASAL CUTTINGS: These come from the bottom of the stem, near where it arises from the parent plant. With English ivy, basal cuttings grow most strongly because the tissue is older and firmer and has a richer supply of stored carbohydrates to fuel root regeneration.

Basal cuttings also work well with hardy perennials. In this case, the cuttings are entire newly emerged shoots, cut off just above the ground. For plants such as yarrow or phlox, they may root better than tip cuttings taken later in the growing season.

LATERAL STEM CUTTINGS: Stems that grow horizontally may have shorter internodes than quick-growing upright stems, which makes for more compact cuttings that are less likely to wilt. Lateral stem cuttings are most successful on plants such as rhododendrons, plums, and white pines.

SEMI-MATURE SUMMER CUTTINGS (ALSO CALLED SEMI-HARDWOOD CUTTINGS): These are cuttings taken in late summer or early fall that have begun to develop a woody stem. They are used to propagate broad-leaved evergreens such as germander (*Teucrium chamaedrys*), English ivy, hollies, rhododendrons, and Fortune's euonymus (*Euonymus fortunei*). Since these evergreens continue to photosynthesize into winter, they can nourish root growth during winter if kept in a heated greenhouse or indoor light garden. Propagation by semi-mature summer cuttings can give you some indoor garden activities to enjoy while the garden outside is covered with a blanket of snow.

wood or root cuttings that can be impossible to tell top from bottom.

When working with foliated cuttings, clear away foliage from the soon-to-be buried portion of the stem; this step is important because it will reduce the risk of rotting. If you have a 2-node cutting, remove the leaves from the lower node and leave the foliage on the upper node. For cuttings that have more than 2 nodes, remove the leaves from the bottom third to half of the cutting.

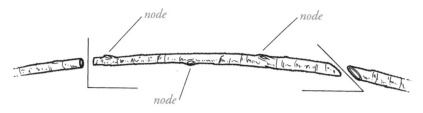

When making hardwood cuttings, angle the lower cut to identify the bottom.

STICKING CUTTINGS: The process of inserting the barren bases of stem cuttings into the growing medium is the turning point that changes slivers of stem into prospective garden plants. If you are planting in open containers, the cuttings can line up in rows, close enough so that the foliage barely touches neighboring cuttings. Plants that are prone to rotting need to be farther apart so they get plenty of free air circulation. Make holes in the rooting medium before inserting the cuttings so that the powdered rooting hormone won't smear off as the cutting pushes through the medium. Finally, firm the rooting medium around the cuttings and label them.

CUTTING CARE: Carefully orchestrating warmth, moisture, humidity, and fertilizer will keep cuttings on track.

Gentle heat between 75° and 80°F, applied beneath the propagating container, can help softwood cuttings root. This is easily accomplished by setting the propagating container on various types of heating cables, available in many garden centers or garden supply catalogs. (For more information on using heating cables, see page 27).

Stick dormant hardwood cuttings taken in spring immediately in well-drained media.

One of the secrets of successful container gardening is maintaining ideal root medium moisture—a quality worth cultivating with your cuttings. The medium needs to be damp and spongy, but not wet and soggy or dry and dusty. When dry, peat moss takes on a faded appearance and the container will feel light. When wet, peat moss will feel oversaturated when you stick your finger beneath the surface. You can

ROOT REGENERATION: BETTER THAN MEDICINE

Stem cuttings rely on a powerful force within plants—totipotency, the fact that plant cells carry a library of genetic information they can call upon to resprout missing roots. Totipotency is like a first-aid kit for plants, but instead of bandaging up broken limbs, they are able to resprout broken or missing parts. For example, willow branches fallen in a shallow pool of water will root to form a thicket of new saplings. A pachysandra shoot, accidentally cut off by an errant swipe of the hoe, can be stuck in damp soil or water to regenerate its lost foundation.

Roots on a cutting usually arise within the stem, just below the severed end. Because of their location, they are called wound roots—

a unique process that brings roots to life on a cutting stem.

When a stem is cut, the outer cells die and seal the opening. Living cells near the seal begin to multiply and form a callus. The callus layer captures sugars produced by the foliage that are transported down the stem and used to nourish new roots. (With hardwood cuttings, stored food reserves replace food created by photosynthesis.)

Hormones in the cutting signal cells near the callus and stem veins to develop into a cell division growth center that can initiate new roots. These roots eventually emerge through the callus or along the base of the cutting, gradually elongating into a web capable of supporting the new plant.

---

estimate moistness of sand and other well-drained media by weight; greater moisture equals greater weight. The medium may not need much water at the beginning of the process. The cuttings will be domed in clear plastic and kept in low light, which help retain moisture. But as rooting proceeds, you should check soil moistness every day and water if needed.

Maintaining high humidity is important for all but very firm, mature cuttings or cuttings prone to rots or other diseases. Plastic tenting and moist soil handle this aspect well. But all cuttings also need some fresh air for healthy foliage. The plastic tent should be removed for a few minutes every day or small ventilation holes should be cut in the plastic top. As the root system matures and the shoots are able to handle lower humidity, the size of the cuts can be increased to larger slits.

Once roots begin to develop, gentle doses of balanced fertilizer

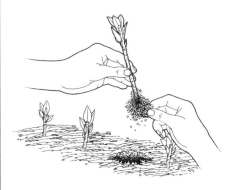

Roots should be about an inch long before transplanting.

provide nutrients that keep cuttings growing strongly, avoiding the lag that will result from nutrient depletion. In a pinch, water soluble fertilizers can be applied to the cutting's foliage for a minor nutrient boost. Fertilization is especially important when propagating herbaceous or softwood cuttings in sterile growing media such as peat moss or sand, which contain little or no natural nutrients.

One option is to water with a half-strength solution of liquid fertilizer every two weeks or, alternatively, to topdress or sprinkle the surface of the growing media with mild, slow releasing granular fertilizer once every month or two.

TRANSPLANTING CUTTINGS: Before cuttings can be potted up, they need sturdy, self-supporting root systems, which can take some time to develop. Basil may take 2 weeks to be ready to transplant, roses may take 6 weeks, and pines may take months.

You'll need a system to evaluate the underground progress roots are making. A gentle pull on the top of the cutting will indicate if rooting has begun—even delicate new roots will provide resistance. (Do not pull too strongly or the roots could come off.) The emergence of a flush of new leaves, generated by the moisture and nutrients drawn in by fledgling roots, is an indicator that rooting has begun. But usually the roots will need more time to develop. You will see their progress indirectly, as cuttings begin to tolerate lower humidity without wilting and growth continues steadily.

When cuttings no longer need high humidity to stay firm or in the case of hardwood cuttings, when they break dormancy, leaf out, and begin growing successfully, unearth one cutting to check its roots. In cell packs, you could look for roots emerging around the drainage holes. In flats, slide your finger into the growing medium, near the corner or edge of the container, and slip it up under the nearest cutting to uproot it. If the roots are nearly 1" long, the cuttings can go into separate containers; if they are growing in cell packs, they can go directly into the garden.

If well rooted, a cutting can be planted directly outdoors.

To transplant, your hand or a trowel can easily pull up clumps of cuttings. Gently separate the bases of neighboring stems by teasing the root systems apart. Transplant them into 4" or even larger pots that will provide more luxurious growing conditions. Fill the pots with either peat-based or a live-soil blend growing mix (see pages 17 and 19). Scoop out a hole in the center deep enough to encompass the entire root system of the cutting. Set the new plant in the new pot at the same depth that it was growing in the old container, and firm the planting mix around the roots. Young transplants may need a brief period of shade if they begin to look droopy.

SOFTWOOD CUTTINGS

The secret to growing great softwood cuttings is to protect the tender stems from wilting. Surround the cuttings with moisture but do not allow the air or rooting medium to be so wet that the cuttings rot.

Start with cuttings that are fully turgid, holding as much moisture as possible. Try to stick those cuttings immediately while they're still plump and fresh. If a delay is inevitable, enclose the cuttings in a plastic bag, and put them in a cool place. The refrigerator is fine for most hardy plants, but warm-season annuals and tropical houseplants may find the refrigerator too cold. Set them in a glass of lukewarm water, and keep them in a shady spot at room temperature.

With succulent plants such as geraniums and cacti, a brief delay actually helps cuttings root better. Letting these cuttings sit out on your counter for a few hours stops the flow of sap from the bottom of the cutting and helps seal the stem so it will root. This practice also helps to discourage rotting.

To prevent moisture loss from rootless cuttings, a high-humidity environment comes in handy. Cover the propagating container with a clear plastic tent that holds moisture inside like a miniature greenhouse. At first, avoid bright sun and heat that accelerates moisture loss, keeping cuttings in indirect light until rooting takes place. As roots begin to emerge and grow, move the cuttings into gradually brighter light. Eventually, you can move rooted sun-loving plants such as chrysanthemums into direct sun, but shade-loving plants such as rhododendrons are best kept in dappled or partial sun.

A good first-time project to try when experimenting with propagating is taking cuttings of a scented geranium. You could take cuttings in late summer or early fall to bring indoors for the winter. Ideal stems are tip cuttings, which will be bushy with leaves from summer's growth. A 2" cutting, which could include as many as 8 or 10 nodes, will work nicely.

Remove the foliage from the bottom half of the stem, leaving one full-size set of leaves near the top and all the young emerging foliage. Each cutting can go into an individual 6" pot filled with equal parts peat

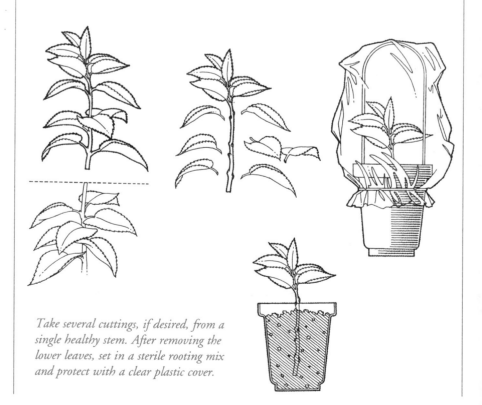

Take several cuttings, if desired, from a single healthy stem. After removing the lower leaves, set in a sterile rooting mix and protect with a clear plastic cover.

PLANTS SUITABLE FOR SOFTWOOD AND HERBACEOUS CUTTINGS

Here is a sampling of the wide variety of plants that you can propagate by softwood cuttings.

ANNUALS AND HOUSEPLANTS

Begonias (*Begonia* spp.)
Coleus (*Coleus* spp.)
Fuchsias (*Fuchsia* spp.)
Geraniums (*Pelargonium* spp.)
Heliotropes (*Heliotropum* spp.)
Hibiscus (*Hibiscus* spp.)
Impatiens (*Impatiens* spp.)
Larkspurs (*Delphinium* spp.)
Wax vines (*Hoya* spp.)

PERENNIALS

Artemisias (*Artemisia* spp.)
Asters (*Aster* spp.)
Bee balms (*Monarda* spp.)
Bellflowers (*Campanula* spp.)
Bergenias (*Bergenia* spp.)
Blanketflowers (*Gaillardia* spp.)
Butterfly weed
    (*Asclepias tuberosa*)
Candytufts (*Iberis* spp.)
Chrysanthemums
    (*Chrysanthemum* spp.)

Dahlias (*Dahlia* spp.)
Hardy geraniums (*Geranium* spp.)
Lavenders (*Lavandula* spp.)
Mints (*Mentha* spp.)
Periwinkles (*Vinca* spp.)
Phloxes (*Phlox* spp.)
Pinks (*Dianthus* spp.)
Plumbagoes (*Ceratostigma* spp.)
Rock cresses (*Arabis* spp.)
Russian sage
    (*Perovskia atriplicifolia*)
Santolinas (*Santolina* spp.)
Speedwells (*Veronica* spp.)
Sundrops (*Oenothera* spp.)
Thymes (*Thymus* spp.)
Yarrows (*Achillea* spp.)

VINES AND GROUND COVERS

Pachysandras (*Pachysandra* spp.)
Virginia creeper
    (*Parthenocissus quinquefolia*)
Wisterias (*Wisteria* spp.)

moss and perlite, which will accommodate the plant through winter.

Cover each pot with a clear plastic bag for several days to a week or until wilting stops. Since rotting can be a problem with scented geraniums, remove the bag as soon as possible and allow the growing medium to dry out slightly before watering again. An east- or west-facing window provides satisfactory light for rooting cuttings, although you may want to keep the cuttings out of direct sun. Once the scented

TREES AND SHRUBS TO PROPAGATE FROM SOFTWOOD CUTTINGS

Abelias (*Abelia* spp.)

Apples (*Malus* spp.)

Barberries (*Berberis* spp.)

Beauty bush
   (*Kolkwitzia amabilis*)

Birches (*Betula* spp.)

Blueberries (*Vaccinium* spp.)

Boxwoods (*Buxus* spp.)

Brooms (*Cytisus* spp.)

Butterfly bushes (*Buddleia* spp.)

Cherries (*Prunus* spp.)

Cinquefoils (*Potentilla* spp.)

Clematis (*Clematis* spp.)

Common lilac (*Syringa vulgaris*)

Cotoneasters (*Cotoneaster* spp.)

Deutzias (*Deutzia* spp.)

Forsythias (*Forsythia* spp.)

Fothergillas (*Fothergilla* spp.)

Fuchsias (*Fuchsia* spp.)

Heaths (*Erica* spp.)

Hibiscus (*Hibiscus* spp.)

Hydrangeas (*Hydrangea* spp.)

Japanese kerria (*Kerria japonica*)

Magnolias (*Magnolia* spp.)

Maidenhair tree (*Gingko biloba*)

Maples (*Acer* spp.)

Mock oranges (*Philadelphus* spp.)

Oregon grape
   (*Mahonia aquifolium*)

Privets (*Ligustrum* spp.)

Roses (*Rosa* spp.)

Russian olive
   (*Eleagnus angustifolia*)

Spireas (*Spirea* spp.)

Trumpet vines (*Campsis* spp.)

Viburnums (*Viburnum* spp.)

Weigelas (*Weigela* spp.)

Willows (*Salix* spp.)

---

geranium is rooted, it will thrive all winter in a brighter south-facing window or fluorescent light garden.

HARDWOOD CUTTINGS

Hardwood cuttings are a great way to grow woody plants without having to juggle humidity or pamper the cuttings indoors. In late fall when all the leaves are raked up, the time is right to take hardwood cuttings. If other projects demand your attention, you can take hardwood cuttings in earliest spring.

Most hardwood cuttings root best from healthy, year-old wood, about the thickness of a pencil. To make sure your favorite plant has plenty of suitable wood to choose from, cut it back hard in early spring and there will be a fresh batch of year-old stems in fall. Alternatively, you could look for year-old stems arising around the base of bushy shrubs and multi-stemmed trees.

It is best to remove entire branches right down to the base when taking hardwood cuttings and to cut them at a 45° angle for future orientation. The angled cut indicates the lower end of the stem. Recut the top of the cutting so it is straight across to avoid confusion. Hardwood cuttings don't dry out as quickly as softwood so they don't need to be stored in plastic bags if you have a brief delay before making and sticking the cuttings.

Hardwood cuttings usually range from 5"–9" long. The cuttings that root most successfully usually come from the base of the branch; the branch tips seldom root. This is because basal cuttings are richer in stored food, important for fueling root growth when foliage is dormant. When making cuttings, place the top cut straight across the stem, ½" or more above the uppermost node or buds. The ½" leeway protects the top buds if the cutting dies back a little during winter.

Since hardwood cuttings are handled when dormant, they need a dose of rooting hormone to get them in the rooting mood. They should be treated with liquid rooting hormones immediately after making them. Bundle similar cuttings together with rubber bands—putting the tops together to preserve proper orientation for winter storage. To prevent the cuttings from drying out and being useless, you can dip the tops in horticultural wax.

Hardy deciduous plants need to receive a period of winter cold before they can leaf out in spring and their cuttings are no different.

VINES SUITABLE FOR HARDWOOD CUTTINGS

Grapes (*Vitis* spp.)
Jasmines (*Jasminum* spp.)
Wisterias (*Wisteria* spp.)

When taken in the fall, cuttings need cold treatment, during which they may appear to be dormant although they're not totally inactive. As winter passes, the bottom of the cutting develops a layer of callus, which is a prelude to rooting.

There are several ways to put hardwood cuttings into winter cold storage, one of which is likely to be convenient for you. In climates with mild winters, you can stick hardwood cuttings directly into rooting medium in a cold frame or even outdoors in a nursery bed. In climates with cold winters, you can put the cuttings in a holding trench, made about 8" deep in well-drained soil. Set the bundled cuttings in the trench horizontally or vertically with tops down and bottoms up; the upside-down method provides more air for the curing bottom cut. Refill the trench, putting several inches of soil over the uppermost portion of the cutting, and then cover the trench with a thick layer of mulch such as straw, corn hulls, or wood chips.

If you have an extra refrigerator that you don't use to store fruits (which release growth hormones in gas form), you could winter hardwood cuttings in it. Put the cuttings in a container of moist sand and keep them at about 50°F for several weeks. Then lower the temperature to slightly above freezing until early spring.

Whether you stick cuttings in the fall in mild climates or early spring in cold climates, the process is the same. You can stick hardwood cuttings directly in nursery beds if the soil is loose, well drained, and sandy. If not, build a raised propagating bed or prepare a cold frame or large nursery pots with equal parts peat moss and perlite or coarse sand. The rooting medium must be as deep as the cuttings are long, which provides a little extra room for root growth.

Space cuttings 4"–6" apart, sticking them so only the uppermost bud emerges from the rooting medium. They must be firmly in place by late winter or early spring so root formation can begin before any foliage emerges. If delayed until after the buds open, chances of successful rooting decline dramatically.

Keep the rooting mix moist while the cuttings are growing. Provide light shade in spring and gradually increase sun exposure as the roots develop. Fertilize cuttings once a month with a balanced, granular fertilizer. In cold climates, a protected site will minimize winter losses. Most cuttings will be well rooted and ready to transplant the following spring.

Examples of naturally occurring hardwood cuttings—the easiest kind to propagate—may sprout up naturally around your yard. Dormant branched twigs cut in early spring to support newly sown peas may begin to root and sprout, taking hold in the fertile goodness of your vegetable garden soil. This would be the rule rather than the exception if you used branches of willows, which have preformed roots within the

TREES AND SHRUBS TO PROPAGATE FROM HARDWOOD CUTTINGS

Andromeda (*Pieris japonica*)
Beauty bush (*Kolkwitzia amabilis*)
Bougainvillea (*Bougainvillea* spp.)
Boxwoods (*Buxus* spp.)
Butterfly bushes (*Buddleia* spp.)
Cotoneaster (*Cotoneaster* spp.)
Crape myrtle (*Lagerstroemia indica*)
Currants and Gooseberries (*Ribes* spp.)
Dawn redwood (*Metasequoia glyptostroboides*)
Deutzias (*Deutzia* spp.)
Dogwoods (*Cornus* spp.)
Elderberries (*Sambucus* spp.)
Euonymus (*Euonymus* spp.)
Firethorns (*Pyracantha* spp.)
Forsythias (*Forsythia* spp.)
Hollies (*Ilex* spp.)
Honeysuckle (*Lonicera* spp.)
Hydrangeas (*Hydrangea* spp.)

Japanese aucuba (*Aucuba japonica*)
Japanese kerria (*Kerria japonica*)
Kolomikta actinidia (*Actinidia kolomikta*)
Mock oranges (*Philadelphus* spp.)
Mountain laurel (*Kalmia latifolia*)
Mulberries (*Morus* spp.)
Osage orange (*Maclura pomifera*)
Poplars (*Populus* spp.)
Potentillas (*Potentilla* spp.)
Privets (*Ligustrum* spp.)
Raspberries (*Rubus* spp.)
Roses (*Rosa* spp.)
Rose of Sharon (*Hibiscus syriacus*)
Spireas (*Spiraea* spp.)
St. John's wort (*Hypericum* spp.)
Virginia creeper (*Parthenocissus quinquefolia*)
Weigelias (*Weigelia* spp.)
Willows (*Salix* spp.)

stems and release their own rooting hormones as well. Another easy rooter is osage orange (*Maclura pomifera*), which was used as a living fence in Colonial times. Posts set in the ground between farm fields would sprout into rows of trees, growing so thickly that cattle could not push their way through. One experienced propagator has rooted 5-foot-long hardwood cuttings of poplars, creating a large, fast-growing tree almost instantly.

One project you could try with hardwood cuttings is to propagate easy rooters in the same landscape bed where you want them to grow. This can produce nice specimens of gray dogwood (*Cornus racemosa*), Cardinal red osier dogwood (*Cornus sericea* 'Cardinal'), and yellow twig dogwood (*Cornus sericea* 'Flaviramea'). Weigelia (*Weigelia florida*), pussy willows (*Salix discolor*), and most other willows will also work nicely with this method.

Take generous-size cuttings, from 8"–12" long with about 4 to 6 nodes. Paint the tops with white latex paint so they are easy to find on a later date. Provide the ordinary dormant season chilling but in spring, stick the cuttings in moist, well-drained soil in a garden bed. The soil needs to be deeply worked so you can insert the cuttings with only the white tip of the stem emerging. Keep them moist while rooting and look for growth in several weeks or a month.

ROOT
CUTTINGS

Root cuttings, like stem cuttings, work because of the ability of a severed plant part to create whatever pieces are missing. Animals have nothing to match this powerful force. Even gecko lizards, which can regenerate lost tails, cannot produce a new lizard from the severed tail.

Root regeneration is a fine art for many of the most successful perennial weeds and a few flowers and shrubs. Dandelions, relieved of their foliage by a hoe, will resprout time and time again from the roots. Oriental poppies, sliced and diced by a rototiller, can sprout into dozens of new plants from the bits of severed root. A sumac, dug and moved to a new garden site, can resprout into a thicket from the severed pieces of root left behind.

These plants take the modest root to new heights. When cut off from the lifeline of the parent plant, their remarkable roots can grow into a new plant. They are truly winners in the natural battle for survival of the fittest.

Taken from sections of young roots that can sprout into new plants, root cuttings are a form of vegetative propagation akin to stem cuttings but with a more limited range of application. Perennial plants that store food reserves in their dormant roots are best for this procedure. Other successful candidates are trees or shrubs, such as lilacs, forsythias, and figs that form thickets of suckers, upright stems arising directly from the roots. Suckers also can be divided from the parent plant, a time-effective alternative discussed in Chapter 5.

Like stem cuttings, root cuttings can produce clones of most parent plants but may not come true if taken from variegated plants with foliage marked white or gold. Likewise, thornless blackberries, which are so easy to harvest, arise clad with thorns when propagated from root cuttings.

Again, as with stem cuttings, you can make many or just a few cuttings from roots. A single alkanet can be multiplied into two dozen new plants with sparkling blue flowers on 5' high stems. They can be grown in masses amid shrubs or naturalized with daylilies and ornamental grasses. A half dozen root cuttings from a rugosa rose could become a small flowering hedge beside your vegetable garden. If you are considering commercial propagation, remember that patented plants are protected by law from unlicensed propagation.

As compared to stem cuttings or divisions, root cuttings often take longer to produce finished plants and work successfully for fewer plants. This is because they have so much more to accomplish to grow independently. Stem cuttings only need to sprout roots. But root cuttings must develop new shoots and new roots. After consuming stored nutrients, they discard the old piece of root from which they sprouted. Root cuttings of euonymus and viburnum, for example, regenerate shoots more easily than roots. The shoots emerge, fed by stored food in the root cutting. Then the new shoots sprout their own roots to become self-supporting. To speed this process, a wily propagator can remove the new shoot and grow it on like a stem cutting, using rooting hormones and bottom heat to encourage new growth.

Despite its shortcomings, root cutting remains an important technique for well-rounded gardeners because it is the only vegetative method for growing certain plants (outside of tissue culture, which requires special laboratory conditions). Root cuttings work well with perennials, such as Oriental poppies, that have long, slender, carrotlike taproots. They also excel with Stokes' asters, alkanet, and cupid's dart, plants that grow in a leafy rosette, or clusters of stemless leaves arising directly from the roots at ground level. Rosettes are tough to divide and impossible to use for stem cuttings. Root cuttings come to the rescue for garden phlox as well, which is prone to stem and foliage pests and diseases that limit its potential for stem cuttings. But phlox roots, unscathed by foliage diseases, allow the propagator to get a healthy start on a new generation.

Anatomy of Root Cuttings

There are as many different types of root systems as there are variations in stems, a diversity easy to notice when working with bareroot perennials. Shipped from nurseries devoid of soil in early spring, bare-root perennials often come as a surprise to unwary gardeners. Upon opening the box, no green plant awaits. Instead, spidery, leathery, or fleshy roots lie dormant in need of prompt planting. The exposed roots vary in thickness and in the arrangement of the root system, which affects their handling if used for cuttings.

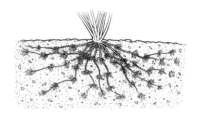

Cuttings of thin or wiry roots can be sown somewhat like seeds.

Variations in Root Thickness: Thin or wiry roots of plants such as phlox are slender and supplemented with little nutrient reserve. With special handling, they can be encouraged to resprout.

Fleshy roots on plants such as cupid's dart and Oriental poppies are thicker, stockpiled with moisture and food reserves, and thus ideal candidates for root cuttings. They can develop more quickly than thin, wiry roots but must be watered sparingly to avoid rotting.

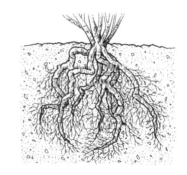

Fleshy roots can be easier to start from root cuttings

Variations in Root System Structure: Always identify which type of root system structure is present in the plants you're propagating *before* you begin. In many cases, the type of root will dictate the method of propagation.

Taproots: Perennials such as Oriental poppies, horseradish, and butterfly weed develop mature carrotlike taproots. These are thick, fleshy main roots that dig deep into the soil, producing smaller side roots along their length. Most taprooted plants don't transplant well because mature

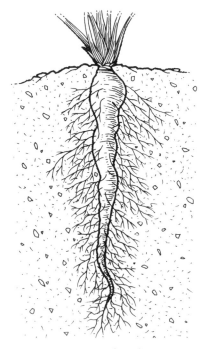

Mature taproots conduct their active feeding at the base of the root, where it can be damaged by digging and transplanting.

taproots are easily disturbed. But some can be sliced into sections to make into cuttings. A favorite children's project is to cut the top off a carrot root and set it in a shallow bowl of water so the ferny greenery will sprout.

FIBROUS ROOTS: Many shrubs, trees, and perennials have fibrous roots, with a netted system of similar-size, branching roots that honeycomb through upper layers of the soil. With plants such as corn, fibrous roots arise from adventitious buds developed at the base of the stem.

CROWN: The point where leafy shoots arise from the roots and emerge from the ground. The best root cuttings often come from sections of root closest to the crown.

MERISTEM: The pocket of unspecialized cells with totipotency, or full genetic memory. They can be switched on to regenerate adventitious buds that replace lost shoots and produce new roots in species suitable for root cuttings.

ADVENTITIOUS BUDS: Suckers that emerge from root cuttings come from adventitious buds, and are generated as a response to the separation from their parent plant. Roots that emerge at the base of newly sprouted stems or stem cuttings emerge from adventitious buds as well.

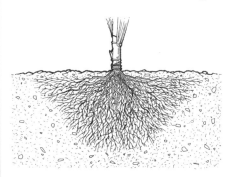

Fibrous roots spread and branch out through the soil.

RHIZOMES: Some perennials have underground stems called rhizomes that closely resemble roots to the casual eye except that they have nodes. They can be propagated similarly to root cuttings, but the procedure is technically a form of division or stem cutting and is discussed in Chapter 5.

TIPS AND TECHNOLOGY

Some additional understanding of the root—how it works and how to make it accessible—is necessary before you can begin root cuttings.

POLARITY: Roots have a remarkable ability to register the effects of gravity, a phenomenon called polarity which tells the roots which side is up. On root cuttings, the lower, or, for horizontally growing roots, outer, end continues to elongate in root growth. The upper, or inner, end, nearest the crown, is the place where new shoots will sprout.

As with stem cuttings, it is important to maintain the root's original orientation when making root cuttings. On all but wire-thin roots this is easily done by making a diagonal cut on the bottom of the cutting and a straight cut on the top. If working with large numbers of root cuttings, bundle them temporarily with tops together and up to avoid accidentally mixing them.

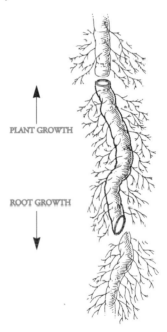

PLANT GROWTH

ROOT GROWTH

Make a diagonal cut at the bottom of the cutting to indicate which end is up.

CULTIVATING PRIME ROOTS FOR CUTTING: Just as you may trim basil plants regularly so they will resprout tender, aromatic new growth for harvesting, you can prepare root systems of multicrowned, clump-forming perennials to produce young, vigorous roots ideal for successful cuttings.

Younger roots may be found only in limited numbers on mature plants. This problem is solved by dividing the root system, which can be a regular aspect of maintaining perennial gardens. Some gardeners divide one-third of their perennials each year so the entire garden is renewed on a three-year cycle. In early spring, the oldest plants are dug, divided into sections, and only the youngest and most vigorous are replanted. They respond by sending out fresh new roots that will be perfect for root cuttings in winter or early spring the following year. Taking root cuttings annually does a similar job, encouraging the plant to develop strong new roots, a harvest for propagating the following year.

CAPTURING THE IDEAL TIMING: Roots have the best potential for regenerating missing parts if taken when the parent plant is dormant and harboring food in the perennial roots. An ideal time falls in late winter or early spring, after hardy perennials have fulfilled their winter cold requirements but before they begin growing again. Cuttings taken and provided with heat can get a jump on the growing season, always a help in cold climates. To be assured access to dormant roots during prime propagating time takes some advance planning.

If herbaceous perennials may be frozen in the ground in late winter or early spring, start in late fall by digging them up. Replant them in a large pot of moist vermiculite, label it with the cultivar name, and submerge the pot in sand or well-drained soil in a cold frame or any protected area near the house. Covering the wintering site with a bale of hay helps keep the soil from freezing solid around the plant. The plant is now easy to bring indoors any time in late winter or early spring.

In areas with mild winters, wet soil might keep you from digging up dormant roots. If wet weather and soggy soil characterize winter in your climate, move the plants to a well-drained raised bed of sandy soil in fall so sloppy soil cannot cause delays and promote disease.

A STRATEGIC SUMMER TIMING EXCEPTION

A few herbaceous perennials, such as Oriental poppies, bleeding heart, and pasque flower, go dormant in summer. This is an easy time to gather their roots without having to deal with frigid or wet soil. When the foliage begins to yellow as the plant prepares to die back, the time is right to harvest the roots you need and make them into root cuttings.

TOOLS: Root cuttings require a few extra tools, above and beyond those needed for stem cuttings.

A sturdy spade, suitable for unearthing parent plants, is required. It must be strong enough to lever under large perennials or small shrubs to help pry them from the earth. It should also have a sharp cutting edge, enabling you to slice off the roots of large sucker-forming shrubs or trees without digging up the entire plant.

An axe or hatchet may also prove useful if you're planning to work with woody roots. When making root cuttings, more refined cutting tools, which can slice through the root without mashing it, are called for. Scissors type pruning shears will work for small woody roots or any size herbaceous roots. A pruning knife also is acceptable for herbaceous roots.

Sterilize cutting tools to avoid spreading diseases before moving from one plant to another, particularly when working with disease-prone plants like blackberries or raspberries. Rub the blades with a rag wet with isopropyl alcohol, Lysol disinfectant, or a 10% bleach solution. When finished for the day, rinsing the blades and drying them well will help prevent corrosion.

GROWING MEDIA AND CONTAINERS: Root cuttings need a substance that will surround, insulate, and protect them from drying out. Gardeners who have stored carrots in moist sand in a root cellar will know that root packing material cannot be too dry—or the roots will shrivel—nor too moist—or the roots will rot. (Some very fleshy roots, such as Chinese forget-me-not and bear's breeches, are extremely prone to rot before they begin to grow. Instead of planting them in anything, some commercial growers pre-sprout them in a climate-controlled sweat-box where they can control rot problems before they spread.) For most roots—sprouted or not—peat moss, perlite, vermiculite, and coarse sand are preferred to true soil, which can be too heavy and may be contaminated with rot-causing pathogens.

Small or fleshy roots can go in pots or flats with a potting medium such as coarse sand or a blend of one part peat moss and one part perlite. Eight-inch bulb pans, shallower than ordinary pots, are large enough to handle over a dozen root cuttings with a little extra space left over. To reuse plastic nursery pots or flats, wash them out with soapy water then sterilize them with a 10% bleach solution to remove pathogens that could infect the root cuttings. If propagating larger roots outdoors, set them in a cold frame filled with coarse sand.

HANDLING DIFFERENT ROOT TYPES: The size of different types of roots influences how to situate them in the growing medium. Here are some examples.

WIRY FIBROUS ROOTS: Treat them carefully, like small seeds. Cut them into modest 1"- to 2"-long pieces and set them horizontally in a pot of sterile rooting mix. Cover shallowly. They will sprout into tiny plants that must be protected from drying out.

FLESHY ROOTS: Cut them into pieces 1"–3" long, and set them upright in propagating mix, retaining their original polarity. Well-drained growing media and care to avoid overwatering is important to prevent rotting.

EXTRA-LARGE ROOTS: Of trees or shrubs for instance, can be 6" long or longer and grown outdoors. The extra root length provides supplemental stored food reserves to nourish slow but steady growth without supplemental heat. To develop the callus that seals the root and prepares it for resprouting, many of these roots need to be cured (a little like hardwood cuttings) in damp sand and 40°F temperatures for several weeks, and then planted in a cold frame or nursery bed to sprout.

ROOT CUTTINGS, BASICS AND BEYOND

Some of the terminology and techniques used for root cuttings are similar to those used for stem cuttings. The biggest difference lies in the nature of the root tissue and the fact that it develops underground.

TAKING CUTTINGS: To remove some of the roots from a plant, begin with finding and unearthing them from the ground. Digging around the perimeter of herbaceous perennials, either at the stem tips or up to 6" beyond, will loosen the surface roots. Slide the spade below the plant, as low as possible and from several directions, to cut free deeper roots that bind the plants to the soil. Use the spade to pry the plant out of the ground.

PLANTS SUITABLE FOR ROOT CUTTINGS

PERENNIALS

Alkanet (*Anchusa azurea*)

Bear's breeches (*Acanthus mollis*)

Blanketflower
(*Gaillardia* × *grandiflora*)

Bleeding hearts (*Dicentra* spp.)

Butterfly weed (*Asclepias tuberosa*)

California poppy
(*Eschscholzia californica*)

Chinese forget-me-not
(*Brunnera macrophylla*)

Crambe (*Crambe cordifolia*)

Cupid's dart (*Catananche caerulea*)

Gas plant (*Dictamnus albus*)

Horseradish (*Armoriacia rusticana*)

Japanese anemones
(*Anemone* × *hybrida* and *A. hupehensis* var. *japonica*)

Leadwort
(*Ceratostigma plumbaginoides*)

Lily turf (*Liriope* spp.)

Oriental poppy
(*Papaver orientale*)

Pasque flower (*Pulsatilla vulgaris*)

Phlox (*Phlox* spp.)

Plume poppies (*Macleaya* spp.)

Stokes' aster (*Stokesia laevis*)

SHRUBS

Bayberry (*Myrica pennsylvanica*)

Bottlebrush buckeye
(*Aesculus parviflora*)

Brambleberries, blackberries, and
raspberries (*Rubus* spp.)

Flowering quinces (*Chamaenomeles japonica* and *C. speciosa*)

Forsythia (*Forsythia intermedia*)

Lilac (*Syringa vulgaris*)

Roses, shrub types (*Rosa* spp.)

Sumacs (*Rhus* spp.)

TREES

Apples and crab apples, ungrafted
(*Malus* spp.)

Black locust (*Robinia pseudoacacia*)

Callery pear (*Pyrus calleryana*)

Fig (*Ficus carica*)

Goldenrain tree
(*Koelreuteria paniculata*)

Japanese pagoda tree
(*Sophora japonica*)

Plums and cherries, ungrafted
(*Prunus* spp.)

Sassafras (*Sassafras albidum*)

Silk tree (*Albizia julibrissin*)

White poplar, Quaking and
European aspen
(*Populus alba* and *P. tremuloides*)

VINES

American bittersweet
(*Celastrus scandens*)

Passion flowers (*Passiflora* spp.)

Trumpet vine (*Campsis radicans*)

You can dig up just one or two roots of a sucker-forming shrub or tree that would be difficult to uproot entirely. Insert a spade into the soil near a young, existing sucker to find the root it arises from. Cut the root free from the plant with the sharp edge of the shovel or with an axe or hatchet. Slide the shovel around and under the root to bring it up out of the ground.

Once the root donor is freed from the earth, gently wash it free from soil and look closely for old, damaged, or diseased sections not worth propagating. Choose young, healthy roots just below where they emerge from the crown. You could take up to one-third of the fibrous roots of herbaceous perennials such as leadworts, bleeding hearts, and phlox. If replanted and kept moist, the parent perennial will recover and continue to perform well in the garden. Taproots, however, generally must be sacrificed, consumed almost entirely for root cuttings.

If you are unable to make and plant cuttings of roots right away, storing them in plastic bags in the refrigerator for a few hours will keep them from drying out. Some fleshy roots, especially Oriental poppies, actually benefit from sitting out in the open if there is a delay. Oriental poppies exude a milky sap that will dry up in fresh air, producing a better quality root for cuttings.

Remove roots near the crown, where food reserves are richest.

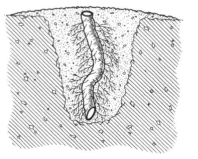

Stick fleshy root cuttings, with respect to their original polarity, near the soil surface.

MAKING ROOT CUTTINGS: To section roots into individual cuttings, begin by trimming the small side roots off fleshy roots or taproots with a sharp knife or pruning shears. After that you can cut the roots into pieces of the proper size: 1" long for wire-thin roots; 1"–3" long for fleshy roots; and up to 6" long for large or woody roots grown outdoors.

PLANTING ROOT CUTTINGS: Set root cuttings into a moist but well-aerated rooting medium that will keep the roots from drying out but won't encourage rotting. Root cuttings of different species develop at different rates; Oriental poppies taken in August sprout within weeks while bleeding heart can take months. It is handy to put each different species in a different container so you can alter light, fertilizer, and transplanting regimes easily. Remember to label them.

Space cuttings at least 1" apart to allow room for root growth and to minimize problems of rotting. Wiry cuttings, without the food reserves to rise through thick layers of growing medium, belong on the surface of moist rooting medium, sprinkled lightly to cover with more rooting medium.

Fleshy and large cuttings grow best if set as nature intended, vertically in the rooting medium with the top just below the surface of the medium. If, however, you grow them in a flat that is too shallow to accommodate the entire cutting, they could be inserted at a slight angle. Use a pencil, wooden rod, or dowel to make a hole in the growing medium that is as deep as the cutting is long. Space holes for fleshy cuttings 1" or 2" apart and insert the root cuttings once all the holes have been made. Space holes for woody cuttings 4"–6" apart in a cold frame or nursery bed.

HORSERADISH

One great plant to propagate by root cuttings is horseradish, which has long fleshy roots full of pungent flavor—a treat in Bloody Marys or roast beef sauce. The zip begins to evaporate the moment the root is cut and grated, making garden-fresh roots potent and well worth growing.

The time to harvest horseradish and take cuttings is in the fall, after the leaves have yellowed and begun to die back. Dig around each plant and carefully unearth the entire root system. Rinse off the roots and harvest the largest for your kitchen. Smaller roots that branch off near the crown make ideal root cuttings. Separate them with a sharp knife and set aside.

Rework the planting bed, loosening the soil, adding extra compost, and smoothing it out. With a wooden dowel, you can make planting holes slightly deeper than the root cuttings, spacing them about 6" apart. Slip in the cuttings, firm the soil around them, and water well. They will begin growing in spring and will be ready to harvest again in fall.

Root Cutting Care: Before root cuttings begin to grow, they use little water. Keeping them slightly dry at that time is preferable to smothering them with excessive moisture. Place the pot in indirect light until growth resumes. Then move the pot to a south-facing window or under fluorescent lights to speed growth. Ordinary household temperatures can be sufficient for root cuttings; for faster results, try providing bottom heat by placing the pot on a heating cable set to 75° or 80°F.

When the first shoot sprouts emerge, growth can be strengthened by misting the shoots with half-strength, balanced, liquid fertilizer. Foliar feeding allows plants to absorb some nutrients through pores in the foliage, even when the roots are not yet established. Once the cuttings are rooted, watering with dilute liquid fertilizer as often as once a week is fine if the cuttings are growing quickly in bright light.

Transplanting Root Cuttings: Once cuttings are well-rooted, they can be moved to their own containers or into the garden. Root cuttings need plenty of time to get off to a strong start, although fleshy roots tend to progress faster than other kinds. When shoots begin growing vigorously, uproot one cutting and see how well established the roots are. If new roots are close to 1" long, you can transplant the cuttings into individual containers of live-soil mix or into a nursery bed (see page 17). If there are no roots, only shoots emerging from the root cutting, you can remove the shoots and root them like you would stem cuttings (see page 78).

DIVISION

ivision, the separation of sections of a spreading plant, like pieces of a pizza, is an ideal method for propagating many kinds of bulbs and perennial plants. It creates several new plants from a single parent plant, depending on the size of the divisions you make, and rejuvenates the parent plant in the process. Like other forms of vegetative propagation, division produces replicas of the parent plant. It can be more effective than stem or root cuttings because divisions reproduce tough-to-clone variegated plants.

Large divisions are immediately garden-ready and, given a few months, may perform better than their parent plant. The speedy recovery of these divisions, which come complete with intact roots and shoots, is one big advantage to this method.

Division does not require special growing mixes, indoor lighting, or greenhouselike conditions. However, it does take some old-fashioned work and muscle. Digging plants, especially large old perennials, can be heavy work best left for someone with a strong back. But sectioning the plants into divisions can provide insight into the nature of each perennial. Looking at the size of the roots, the way they emerge from the crown, and how far they spread will further your understanding of why a species grows as it does.

The only drawback of division is that it doesn't work well for every plant. Perennials that grow into a leafy rosette with a single crown, like Stokes' aster, or that sprout from a taproot, like Oriental poppies, can be difficult or impossible to divide. Likewise, plants with woody roots—

found in the aging center of some perennial clumps or in most trees and shrubs—can be slow to rebound from division and are best propagated by other means.

Like stem and root cuttings, divisions need to be taken from disease-free plants so that problems will not be passed along to progeny. They also should come from gardens with healthy soil because soil-bound divisions transplanted to other gardens can spread diseases and pests.

ANATOMY OF DIVISION

Successful division relies on observing a plant's anatomy and determining if it has the right components for propagating by this method. Taking a rabbit's-eye view on hands and knees will provide most of the information you need.

Crown: This is the point where leafy shoots arise from the roots and emerge from the ground. Plants with multiple crowns are suitable for division. A well-grown daylily, for example, may have 50 crowns, or fans, of leaves arising in a large plant clump. The plant could be separated into 50 small pieces, 10 medium pieces, or 3 large pieces.

Each leafy sprout on a daylily can be separated into a new plant.

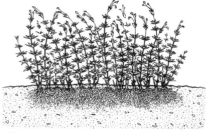

Some perennials creep on fibrous roots and are easily divided.

Fibrous roots: Many perennials have fibrous roots, with a branching system of similar-size roots that honeycomb upper layers of the soil. These roots are suitable for separation by division, unlike taproots.

Creeping growth: Plants with spreading stems (called rhizomes or stolons) sprout shoots and roots as they wander and can cover a broad territory. Spearmint, for example, can spread up to 4' or 5' a year but is easy to divide for size control and propagation.

Rhizomes/Stolons: Creeping stems that grow under the ground are called rhizomes; those that

Vines such as ivy root as they grow, providing plenty of opportunity for division.

grow on the ground are called stolons. They closely resemble roots to the casual eye but contain budded nodes, which are capable of sprouting into leaves and shoots. If you have planted bare-root lily-of-the-valley or harvested the pips (budded rhizomes) to force into flower in winter, you've seen thick rootlike rhizomes, perfect mimics of true fleshy roots. Newly purchased cannas and bearded iris start from such large fleshy rhizomes that you might think they were bulbs. Bamboos, some of which spread like lightning, are able to do so with the help of quick-growing rhizomes.

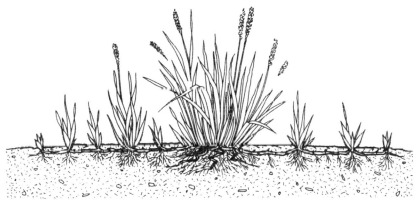

Seemingly independent grasses emerge from spreading underground stems.

Although rhizomes are stems, they can be propagated using root-cutting techniques, or they can be allowed to sprout in spring and divided with their roots and shoots already onboard. Rhizomes are easy to separate with the blade of a sharp spade.

Other underground stems: Instead of funneling resources to the roots in preparation for dormancy, some perennials modify underground stems to stockpile food reserves and buds for future growth. The anatomy of these structures is slightly different and affects the way they are divided.

Bulbs are actually modified stems capable of multiplying.

Bulbs: Easy to recognize in garden center bins in fall, bulbs are sections of stem with food-storing leaves surrounding a budded embryo. Bulbs may have a single set of fleshy leaves that makes them appear solid, like a tulip, or like an onion, they may be composed of multiple fleshy leaves and look layered.

At the base of the bulb, deep within its heart, new bulbs are initiated and nurtured to expand the range of the original bulb. Sometimes new bulbs replace the original bulb altogether, which is the case with tulips. Sometimes they spread out beside the original bulb. When new bulblets grow large enough to handle, they are easily propagated by snapping them off and growing them on in a nursery bed until they are large enough to flower.

THE LIFE OF A BULB

Daffodil bulbs, bought with a single nose, contain one set of fragrant golden flowers nice enough for the first year. Provided with plenty of cool spring weather, lots of sun, and foliage left free until it yellows, a single bloom can multiply into many, which may be the only way to make a good daffodil even better.

Year One: A single-nose daffodil bulb conceives a bulblet, which is called a split.

Year Two: The split bulblet hangs onto the side of the parent bulb, making a two-nosed bulb with two sets of flowers and twice the bloom.

Year Three: The first split separates from the parent down to the root plate, where it remains attached. Another split will arise, providing three sets of flowers.

Future Years: After multiplying repeatedly, daffodils can get overcrowded. In fact, it's not unheard of that they may stop flowering altogether. By dividing all the young bulbs and enriching the garden soil, the process can begin all over again.

Corms: Plants such as crocus and gladiolus grow from corms, which look similar to bulbs but have subtle differences. Instead of being surrounded with fleshy leaves, a corm is a swollen stem, often wrapped in dry, protective leaves that form a brown skin. At the top of the rounded corm

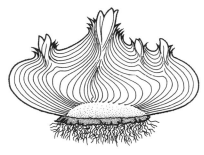

Professionally sectioned corms can develop into several new plants.

(rather than inside), buds develop into shoots and flowers. At the bottom, buds become roots. Other, undeveloped buds may lie dormant on the sides of the corm, resting there as long as the corm is whole. Commercial growers make use of these buds by sectioning a large corm into several pieces, which jump-starts side buds to replace lost shoots and roots.

The gladiolus arises from a corm that expends all its reserves supporting the tall spikes of colorful, trumpet-shaped flowers. After flowering, sunshine and fertile soil allows the plant to produce a replacement corm that will flower the following year. A handful of mini corms, flowering wannabes, develop around the base of the largest corm. They can be broken off and nurtured for a year or two until they reach flowering size.

Tubers: Yet another form of swollen stem, the tuber grows beneath Irish potatoes, Jerusalem artichokes, elephant ears, tuberous begonias, and cyclamen. Tubers have distinct eyes or buds along the length of the tuber, instead of

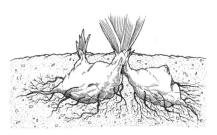

An iris grows from a fleshy rhizome — also a modified stem.

clustered like a corm, with buds that appear at the top or bottom. This allows for extra-easy propagation.

When planting Irish potatoes, the tubers can be cut into pieces containing at least one bud each to provide up to a half-dozen new plants from one tuber. But since cutting the tuber open can invite rotting, Irish potatoes need to sit in warm temperatures for several days to seal the openings with a protective callus before planting. Once submerged in warm, well-drained soil, new sprouts soon emerge, growing quickly and consuming the energy stored in the tuber, which shrivels away. As the plants mature, they produce spreading underground stems that sprout clusters of new tubers for the next season.

Dahlias have tuberous roots, which swell like potatoes but have no buds and cannot grow independently. To divide dahlias, the crown that contains the buds must be divided so that each piece of crown contains a bud and a tuberous root.

TIPS AND TECHNOLOGY

A person blessed with a green thumb is simply a prepared gardener who has planned in advance for every contingency. Putting some forethought into when to accomplish the tasks and having the right tools on hand when it is time to take action are the two most important components to success.

TOOLS: Division requires the same tools as root cuttings—spades for unearthing roots and possibly a hatchet for cutting through woody roots. Pruning shears or a pruning knife come in handy, too, when separating divisions, as well as do two sturdy garden forks. When set back-to-back in the middle of a perennial clump, they can be pulled apart to separate the roots.

GOOD TIMING: Time works to your advantage if you can wait until the beginning or end of the growing season to divide. But with easily divided plants such as daylilies, almost any timing decision you make is the right one.

To put divisions directly in the ground with minimal fuss and bother, you should divide when the weather is mild and moist so plants can generate lavish roots before extreme heat or cold strikes. In cold climates, divisions made in the spring have the entire growing season to get established before winter arrives. Spring has added advantages for newly divided plants because they are growing vigorously, fueled by stored food reserves, and may be able to get established faster.

Fall often works well for divisions because the cooler weather limits the demands on the root system. In warm climates, fall provides many months of moderate weather before the heat of summer tests new root systems. Loss of foliage at this time of year, though slightly premature, is not a major drain, unlike in summer.

Summer is an ideal time to divide spring-blooming plants that rest in summer, including German irises, old-fashioned bleeding heart, tulips, and daffodils. For other perennials, summer may be a difficult time for division. If it is the only option—perhaps an irrepressible inspiration strikes—you should cut perennials foliage back by half to balance root loss while the plant becomes reestablished.

The choice between spring and fall may come down to flowering time. Imagine the consequences of uprooting a tomato just as the fruit is beginning to ripen—the results are likely to be disastrous. Likewise, dividing a cherished perennial in mid bloom is likely to make the display disappointing. To maximize garden beauty and minimize unnecessary stress, try to avoid dividing for several months before bloom. Spring bloomers should be divided in late summer or fall, and summer bloomers in spring.

DIVISION BASICS

L earning the technique for division will serve you well in many ways. It will multiply your plants and could increase your circle of friends as well. Plants that need regular division for routine maintenance are likely to produce more offspring than one garden can handle. Giving extras to friends or swapping them at organized perennial exchanges—with warnings, of course, about the nature of rampant spreaders—makes use of every piece.

In an established perennial garden, division is a wonderful reorganizational tool. A great new cultivar of yarrow with pastel salmon flowers can be nursed into maturity in a relatively obscure location, then divided into 3 or 5 plants that can move into the mainstream as an attention-drawing sweep of color. Hostas, with waffled blue leaves the size of dinner plates, may well be forgotten beneath an old oak tree. But when divided and set here and there in a partly shaded perennial garden, the foliage becomes dynamic. It provides rhythm through the garden and a bold, tropical look that contrasts nicely with narrow straplike daylily leaves or divided, lime green goatsbeard leaves.

Division should not consume much of your time. In a single afternoon, you can divide and replant a half-dozen plants. But it does require some advance planning and effort to move swiftly once the plants are out of the ground. Here is the process for making successful divisions.

Planning Ahead: The inspiration for dividing a plant often comes during quiet contemplation of the garden in full bloom. When one flower looks great, it is natural to want more so the entire garden can look the same. Now's the time to note that thought and tag the plant so it will be easy to find in fall or spring, when the time is right for division.

As dividing time draws closer, a place must be prepared to receive new divisions. Whether in an established garden or a new garden, existing vegetation must be cleared away. The soil should be amended with organic matter such as compost and loosened at least 8"–10" deep to accommodate a deeply dug root system. The root ball should not emerge awkwardly from the soil, nor should roots be crammed or curled into a hole that's too small. This may mean loosening deep-down soil with a spade or garden fork in addition to rototilling the surface soil. Careful soil preparation will bring rewards in good growth for years to come.

Unearthing the Plant: Before clumps of perennials or bulbs can be divided, the roots must come up and out of the ground. Digging around the perimeter of the perennial with a spade—either at the perimeter of the foliage or beyond—will loosen the roots. Sliding the spade beneath the plant from several directions will break the root ball free. Plants such as thyme and coral bells are shallow rooters that can be unearthed with minimal effort. But daylilies, hostas, and peonies can send roots deep—several feet or more—and will become reestablished rapidly if dug as deeply as possible. Because this can be a heavy job on a big plant, you can cut the plant into several pieces before uprooting it to save wear and tear on your back.

If there is open space in the garden beside the uprooted plant, it may be handy to slide it off the spade there and continue with the next phase of division. If not, you can put it on the lawn, but you'll have to rake clumps of soil back into the garden when you are through. Alternatively,

PERENNIALS AND THEIR DIVISION PREFERENCES

A good time to propagate perennials is when they need division for routine maintenance.

Many of the best garden perennials grow at a moderate pace—steady but not excessively aggressive. They can be divided every 3 or 4 years, or when the plant clump grows large enough to be unruly or shabby and the soil is in need of enrichment with organic matter.

DIVIDE EVERY YEAR OR TWO

Artemisia (*Artemisia ludoviciana* 'Silver King'; quick spreader)

Asters (*Aster* spp.; require frequent rejuvenation)

Bee balms (*Monarda* spp.; quick spreaders)

Chrysanthemums (*Chrysanthemum* spp.; require frequent rejuvenation)

Gooseneck loosestrife (*Clethera alnifolia*; quick spreader)

Mints (*Mentha* spp.; quick spreaders)

DIVIDE EVERY 3 TO 4 YEARS

Bearded iris (*Iris* × *germanica*)

Catmint (*Nepeta mussinii*)

Chives (*Allium schoenoprasum*)

Coreopsis (*Coreopsis* spp.)

Fernleaf yarrow (*Achillea filipendulina*)

French tarragon (*Artemisia dracunculus* var. *sativa*)

Garden phlox (*Phlox paniculata*)

Lady's mantle (*Alchemilla vulgaris*)

Reblooming daylilies (*Hemerocallis* 'Stella d'Oro')

Sea thrift (*Armeria maritima*)

Sneezeweed (*Helenium autumnale*)

Thymes (*Thymus* spp.)

Violet sage (*Salvia* × *superba*)

DIVIDE EVERY 5 TO 10 YEARS, IF NEEDED

Astilbes (*Astilbe* spp.)

Epimediums (*Epimedium* spp.)

Hardy geraniums (*Geranium* spp.)

Hostas (*Hosta* spp.)

Lungworts (*Pulmonaria* spp.)

Peony (*Paeonia officinale*)

Sedum (*Sedum* × 'Autumn Joy')

Siberian iris (*Iris sibirica*)

SELDOM OR NEVER DIVIDE

Balloonflower (*Platycodon grandiflorus*)

Baptisia (*Baptisia australis*)

Christmas rose (*Helleborus niger*)

Gas plant (*Dictamnus albus*)

Globe thistle (*Echinops ritro*)

Lovage (*Levisticum officinale*)

Monkshood (*Aconitum* spp.)

Oriental poppy (*Papaver orientale*)

Rue (*Ruta graveolens*)

Sea lavender (*Limonium latifolium*)

you could put the root ball in a wheelbarrow, garden cart, or a sturdy box or flat to move to a more convenient workplace.

Methods for separating and transplanting the divisions will vary according to whether you are working with perennials or bulbs, depending on their respective growth habits.

DIVIDING PERENNIALS: If dividing perennials in summer or fall, when the leaves are fully grown, cutting stems back by one-half or two-thirds of their total length will minimize wilting. It is unnecessary to cut

back foliage if you are dividing plants in spring when the newly arising shoots are not yet unfurled and are easy to work around without disturbing them. Large divisions of durable plants such as daylilies or hostas sometimes withstand transplanting fully foliated if the weather is cool and the planting site is kept moist.

Some divisions can even be worked apart by hand.

'Stella d'Oro' daylilies, quick growers that benefit from division every couple of years, are especially easy to unearth. Their roots can dwell well below a spade's depth. To capture as many roots as possible, force the spade deeply into the ground at a slight angle under the plant, forcing the spade shoulders down if necessary to extend it to its full depth. With a bracing foot on the spade shoulder, rock the spade up and a portion of

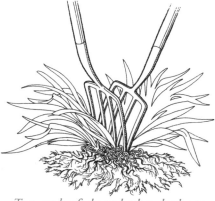

the plant with as many as 20 rooted crowns (which in daylily circles are called fans) will separate off in a large division. The root ball is molded to the shape and depth of the spade, making it easy to fit into a transplanting hole dug with the same spade.

Divison is a wonderful way to maintain control of aggressively spreading plants, like mints and

Two garden forks set back-to-back can pry plants apart.

bee balm, while keeping them healthy and tidy. Mints and bee balm spread on quick-growing, underground stems, appropriately called runners. Their habit is to root as they go, producing dozens of new rooted sprouts in the process. If allowed to spread unchecked, they will cover lots of territory in little time and can overwhelm nearby plants.

If divided each spring, these plants can be contained to a certain extent. As the leaves begin to swell in spring, slip a shovel under the main plant clump. Lever it out of the ground and gently tease up all the rooted stolons that are connected to it. If any snap off, it won't take long for them to grow into new plants. You can hoe or rake through the garden soil to comb out any stolon stragglers. Then separate off a small section of the parent plant, refresh the soil with some compost, and replant. Save the divisions for friends or put them in herbal tea or potpourri.

If only one division is needed—for instance, a fast-spreading 'Silver King' artemisia or a specimen perennial such as a variegated hosta—slicing a wedge off a multicrowned plant works beautifully. Instead of digging up the entire root system, you can carve off an outer piece of the plant. Push a spade into the plant to separate off a wedge and work it carefully between leafy crowns to

A firm slice with a shovel will cut most perennials apart.

minimize damage to the foliage, keeping the parent plant tidy and handsome. Loosen the perimeter of the wedge and with a foot on the shoulder of the spade, rock the spade up to break the plant free.

Once the roots are out in the open, they are ready to separate into divisions. The nature of this procedure depends on how many divisions you want. For many small divisions, the soil should be washed off the roots. Roll the root ball back and forth along the ground to break off excess soil, then use a hose to gently rinse the roots clean. With a garden knife or pruning shears, carefully cut the crown so that each piece includes at least one set of shoots and roots. If the day is hot and sunny, you can protect the roots from desiccation by working in the shade and keeping unattended roots under a damp canvas.

To make a few large divisions, leave the roots encased in soil. Plants without woody crowns may be teased apart by hand. Grasping two sides of the root ball, gently apply pressure to break it into pieces. If more pressure is needed, use two garden forks pushed into the center of the plant, back-to-back. Pull the handles apart to pry the roots apart. If the roots are massive or woody, use a sharp spade, or even an axe, to cut them into pieces.

Replant the divisions immediately, putting large, healthy clumps back into the garden bed. Very small divisions may go into pots of live-soil mix until they grow large enough to go back into the garden. In either case, replant at the same depth that the plants were growing previously unless you are planting in a newly prepared bed. In that case, you should plant slightly deeper so the plant will be at the right level when the tilled soil settles.

Young daffodil bulbs can be snapped loose from the mother bulb.

The water your new divisions need may be provided by nature in the spring or fall. But if rainfall falls short of 1" a week anytime during the season following dividing, you need to irrigate. Mulching around the plants with several inches of organic matter such as compost or shredded bark helps keep the soil cool and moist. If the divisions are small, remove any flowers that arise during the growing season to allow the plant to concentrate energy into growth and reestablishment.

DIVIDING BULBS AND THEIR KIN: If a cluster of daffodils grows into a large sweep and slowly stops flowering, it probably needs division to space out bulbs and refresh the soil. Spring-flower-

Scales on lilies can be separated and grown into a mini bulb.

ing bulbs should be divided in summer, when the foliage yellows but before it dies back entirely. (The foliage tells you where to dig without slicing into the bulbs.) Dig on a dry day when the excess soil can be gently brushed off the bulbs. Most bulbs and corms are easy to break apart by hand, snapping the new bulbs off the parent bulbs. They can be replanted immediately or stored until fall.

Summer storage is appealing because it gives you time to work the soil and plant annuals without damaging bulbs below. In preparation for storage, you should separate bulbs by cultivar or flower color and put them in paper bags labeled with each cultivar name. They must be kept in a cool, airy place until the temperature drops in fall and garden centers begin advertising autumn bulbs. These indicators mean the season is perfect for replanting.

BULBS AND CORMS FOR DIVISION

Bulbs and corms that readily naturalize or multiply in the garden are easy to divide simply by separating off the young plants. Here are some examples.

Crocuses (*Crocus* spp.)
Daffodils (*Narcissus* spp.)
Grape hyacinths (*Muscari* spp.)
Snowdrops (*Galanthus* spp.)
Squills (*Scilla* spp.)
Stars of Bethlehem
   (*Ornithogalum* spp.)
Tulips, species types (*Tulipa* spp.)

Tender, summer-flowering bulbs (also tubers and other underground stems) such as gladiolus, elephant ears, dahlias, and tuberous begonias can be unearthed in the fall, before the foliage is blackened by frost. They should be stored indoors in a cool basement in cardboard boxes filled with peat moss to protect the tender bulbs and to keep them from touching each other. To remind you which bulb is which, label the boxes with the cultivar name or description. In the spring, shortly before planting, divide the tubers or break off new offshoots, bulbs, corms, and other natural propagules. Let tubers cure and callus in an airy place for several days before replanting.

Lilies, also a kind of bulb, do not encase their fleshy food-filled leaves (called scales) in a skin, as do onions or daffodils. They leave them out in the open, making the bulbs look a little like pinecones. Each scale, when separated from the bulb, can develop a mini bulb at its base.

Mini bulbs take several years to become large enough to flower but are a great way to multiply expensive, elite cultivars, or provide an eye-opening experience to share with children.

Begin by removing the scales (a form of division or stem cutting), cutting them with a knife close to the base. Plant them in a cell pack filled with moist vermiculite, one per cell. Push the bottom half of the scale under the surface of the vermiculite and cover with a clear plastic bag. Development proceeds very quickly if the scales are kept at 70°F for 2 months or until the mini bulbs are well grown. If you are propagating during the fall or early winter when lily bulbs need a cold rest period, put the cell pack in the refrigerator for 2 months. Transplant the mini bulbs and set in a light garden or protected outdoor nursery bed to grow on during the ordinary growing season.

LAYERING

ayering is a form of propagation that occurs when a branch is rooted while still connected to the parent plant. The process resembles stem cuttings but is easier. Most commonly, the stem is bent to the ground, nicked on the bottom to encourage rooting, and buried. With the exception of some variegated plants, the progeny is a clone of the parent. Forsythia layers naturally—with its arching branches that root almost promiscuously where they touch the ground—to produce a golden-flowered thicket of identical shrubs.

Used primarily for propagating woody plants, layering does not affect the parent plant, save for the stem or stems devoted to the project. It is almost always done outdoors, with no special equipment and little concern about wilting, hardiness, or hardening off. A gardener can easily layer several plants right in their landscape beds, often with very little fuss or bother.

The number of plants that can be created by layering is limited compared to other forms of propagation because only one offspring arises from each layered stem. This limits layering as a commercial propagating technique but is suitable for the home gardener who doesn't require many new plants. Modified layering techniques allow several stems to be rooted at the same time or one long vine stem to be rooted in several different locations.

Layered stems vary in how long they take to root, but as a rule they progress more slowly than stem cuttings. Tip-layered trailing blackberries take about a month to be prepared for transplanting. The wait

PLANTS TO PROPAGATE BY LAYERING

Apples (*Malus* spp.)

Bellflowers (*Campanula* spp.)

Blueberry, lowbush
  (*Vaccinium angustifolium*)

Clematis (*Clematis* spp.)

Cranesbills (*Geranium* spp.)

Deutzias (*Deutzia* spp.)

Euonymus (*Euonymus* spp.)

Filberts and Hazels (*Corylus* spp.)

Forsythias (*Forsythia* spp.)

Grape, muscadine
  (*Vitis rotundifolia*)

Hawthorns (*Crataegus* spp.)

Honeysuckle (*Lonicera* spp.)

Hydrangeas (*Hydrangea* spp.)

Ivies (*Hedera* spp.)

Jasmines (*Jasminum* spp.)

Magnolias (*Magnolia* spp.)

Mock orange
  (*Philadelphus coronarius*)

Pears (*Pyrus* spp.)

Pinks (*Dianthus* spp.)

Quince (*Cydonia oblonga*)

Rhododendrons (*Rhododendron* spp.)

Roman chamomile
  (*Anthemis nobilis*)

Roses (*Rosa* spp.)

Rosemary, prostrate (*Rosmarinus
  officinalis* 'Prostratus')

Smoketree (*Cotinus coggygria*)

Spireas (*Spiraea* spp.)

Thymes (*Thymus* spp.)

Winter savory (*Satureja montana*)

Wisterias (*Wisteria* spp.)

increases to a few months for layered gooseberries or air-layered ficus and a few years for a magnolia. But so little effort is needed—even for the magnolia—that the time it takes requires little more than patience.

There are several different ways to accomplish layering, although the basic principles are the same for all. Techniques vary according to the needs of specific plants or the number of new plants desired.

A treated, buried stem is nourished by the mother plant while rooting.

Once roots develop, the new plant can be cut free.

GROUND OR SIMPLE LAYERING: This traditional form of layering is suitable for use on a wide variety of woody plants. It begins with a flexible, low-lying branch. The tip of the branch is preserved to become the new plant. The stem just below the tip is stripped of leaves for approximately 5", or long enough to submerge and completely cover with soil. Before planting, the bark is nicked or stripped on the bottom of the stem—the side that will be lowest when buried. Then the stem is submerged and pinned in place, with the stem tip emerging upright and becoming the new plant.

COMPOUND LAYERING: Long flexible vine stems, using ground-layering techniques, can be woven in and out of the ground to produce several layered offspring.

Trailing blackberries naturally submerge stem tips to produce new plants.

TIP LAYERING: This method of reproduction takes advantage of special adaptations in the stem tips of trailing blackberries, dewberries, boysenberries, and black and purple raspberries. The year-old branches arch to the ground, sinking the tip in the soil. The stem tip then sprouts into a new plant that can be cut free in fall or early spring and replanted wherever needed.

MOUND OR STOOL LAYERING: Commercial nurserymen use this system to produce apple, pear, quince, currant, and gooseberry rootstocks, which are bases for grafting buds or stems of great-fruiting, disease-resistant, compact, or other cultivars. When selecting a parent plant, make sure it is grown on its own roots and is a good cultivar in its own right. Many small apple trees, for instance, are grown on dwarfing rootstock that may not

PLANTS TO PROPAGATE BY TIP LAYERING

Blackberries, trailing (*Rubus* spp.)
Boysenberries (*Rubus* spp.)
Dewberry (*Rubus caesius*)
Raspberries, black and purple
    (*Rubus idaeus* and
    R. occidentalis)

produce quality apples. Crab apples, quinces, currants, and gooseberries are easier to find on their own roots than apples and pears. Mound layering will also work with forsythia, honeysuckle, roses, and wisteria.

The entire plant is devoted to the layering process. Allowed to grow for a year after planting, the plant is cut back hard the following spring. As new stems emerge and grow, the bottom half of the plant is covered with sandy soil.

Every stem is covered and encouraged to root when mound layering.

Vigorous and young, these stems will produce roots by the end of the growing season or the following spring and can be severed and transplanted at that time. The parent plant can be used the same way again the next year.

AIR LAYERING: This process is performed primarily on lanky houseplants such as rubber trees that have developed barren stem bases but have upright growth that will not bend to the ground. The stem is girdled, removing a ring of bark to help initiate rooting, then the wound is wrapped in sphagnum moss and a protective outer covering to encourage and protect new roots.

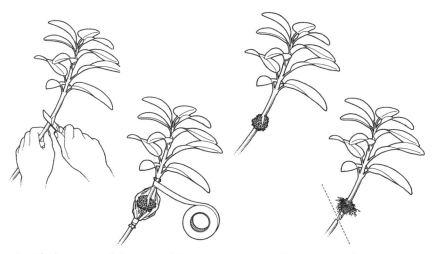

A nicked stem, carefully wrapped in spagnum moss and kept consistently moist, can root and become a new plant.

TIPS AND TECHNOLOGY

With the mother plant continuing to nourish the layered start, no high-tech equipment is needed for layering. Instead, good old-fashioned gardening basics—finding young, healthy stems at the right season of the year—is what's most important.

TIMING: Ground layering works best if started in late winter or early spring, just before plants begin active growth. Fall is also an option although the best results are likely to come from spring starts. Young but firm stems, 1 to 2 years old, offer the best possibility for rooting. Older wood is less likely to root or be flexible enough to bend down to the ground without breaking.

Late summer is the time for tip layering. Year-old stems (also called canes) of trailing blackberries, boysenberries, black and purple raspberries, and dewberries will show their readiness by producing elongated cane tips with small, curled leaves.

TOOLS: Few tools are required for layering. A hoe may be necessary to loosen the soil beside the plant to make a place for the layered stem. A sharp pruning knife is needed to make an incision in the stem or scrape off the bark where the roots are to grow. A garden staple, used to secure floating row covers to the ground, a forked stick, or a flat stone can be used to hold the submerged stem in place. A bamboo stake, inserted beside the emerging stem tip, provides support to keep the tip growing upright into a shapely new plant. Strips of old nylon hose or florist's tape will hold the stem gently to the stake.

ROOTING HORMONES: Hormones called auxins are responsible for initiating rooting in layered stems. Actively growing stems produce their own auxins, which promote rooting in naturally layered black raspberries and prostrate rosemary. When making your own layered plants, it is worth investing in rooting hormones to be sure the process runs smoothly. It is particularly helpful for difficult-to-root plants like magnolias and rhododendrons.

Rooting hormones should be applied after wounding the stem but before putting it in the ground. Powdered rooting hormones can be dusted into openings in the bark. Moistening the bare tissue before applying the hormone can help the powder stick, if you're careful to avoid caking. Excess auxin can deter growth. Long-strand sphagnum moss can be soaked in liquid rooting hormone and slipped into or around stem wounds. For more details on the types and care of rooting hormones, see Chapter 3.

LAYERING BASICS

The general practices developed to encourage the emergence of roots from an intact or almost intact stem can be applied to all the different types of layering.

SITE PREPARATION: The ideal rooting site for the layered stem is close to the plant—so that there is no danger of breaking the stem—and, if possible, in afternoon shade to help keep the soil cool.

Like a good potting mix, the garden soil must be light, well aerated, and moist. Where native soils tend to stay wet, prepare a raised site that will shed excess rainwater. Add abundant peat moss or compost and coarse sand to heavy soil to bring it to a consistency similar to live mixes. Or, instead of amending the soil, you can replace it with a blend of equal parts peat moss and vermiculite. For dry sandy soil, adding abundant compost will help to keep the area cool and moist.

Break up and amend the soil to 6" or 8" deep, using a hoe or trowel to make holes 3" deep with gently curving sides. Holes for tip-layered plants need to be carefully prepared (see opposite page). If the soil is dry, moisten it before proceeding with your stem preparation.

STEM PREPARATION: For simple and compound layering, find a young flexible stem. With a sharp pruning knife—one that will slice through plant tissue without tearing—clear the stem of leaves where it is to be buried, cutting the foliage cleanly off the stem. Identify which side of the stem, when bent to the ground, will be on the bottom. This is the side that will produce roots. Scrape or cut off the bark on that side in a 1"- to 2"-long patch to dam up nutrients and growth hormones. Make sure all the phloem tissue in the bark is removed down to the wood beneath, then apply the rooting hormone.

To prepare tip-layered trailing blackberries, remove any large leaves near the modified stem tip that will be submerged. No rooting hormones are needed. Mound- or stool-layered plants require special preparation throughout the growing season (see page 111).

SUBMERGING AND SECURING THE LAYERED STEM: Gently maneuver the stem into the prepared hole and cover firmly with soil. Layered stems will need to be held in place so wind or passing children and animals will not pull the stem free. Earth staples are easy to push down over the stem and will hold it firmly in the ground with one metal leg on each side of the stem. Tent stakes, angled pegs, or branched sticks can do the same job, albeit they require a little more maneuvering. Some propagators anchor stems with a rock or a brick, which, like mulch, helps keep the soil below moist and cool.

Allow stem tips on all but compound and tip-layered plants, to continue to grow upright. Set a bamboo stake beside the submerged stem if it is growing horizontally or at an angle. Tie the stem loosely to the stake with strips of nylon hose or florist's tape.

TIP LAYERING

For tip layering, only the stem tip is buried. To discourage further growth and reprogram the stem for root development, make the far end of the planting hole into a firm, upright wall. Slope the stem down into the hole and slam the tip up against the firm back wall. Cover and peg down the stem.

LAYERING CARE: The vital element for rooting is moist soil. Similar to rooting stem cuttings, the soil must be damp enough to protect tender, tiny new roots but not so wet that the stem rots. Covering the planting area with 1" of compost or 2" of straw or bark mulch helps to slow moisture loss in dry weather. A soaker hose or trickle irrigation system, turned on automatically with a timing mechanism, can keep the propagating stems and other plants satisfied if you are vacationing during hot or dry weather.

TRANSPLANTING ROOTED LAYERS: After one month or possibly more, depending on the plant being layered, if the tip of a ground layered stem has continued growing steadily, it may be rooted. Pull out the peg holding the stem down and gently tug to feel if the roots are providing any resistance. Avoid pulling too hard—new roots are easily torn. If rooting has begun, brush away the surface soil to identify the extent of the rooting. If the roots have spread to hold a ball of soil 4" or more across, they should be able to support the plant.

Tip-layered trailing blackberries will send up a new shoot, a good indication of successful rooting. Once the shoot becomes substantial, the parental branch can be cut free, leaving a flag of old stem emerging 4" or 5" above the ground to mark the location. The new plant can be moved in the fall or early spring.

Before transplanting, moisten the soil so the earth will cling to the roots and protect them during transport. Using a pruning knife or pruning shears, cut the rooted stem free from the parent plant. Dig a trench around the outside of the root system, and slide the spade underneath to unearth the root ball. Move the plant directly to another part of the garden. If the roots are smaller than expected, plant it in a pot of live-soil mix to nurture it until the roots are large enough to be self-supporting. If the new plant begins to wilt, cut the stems back by up to half of their total height to reduce moisture requirements, tent the plant in a clear plastic dome, and place it in light shade until it's fully recovered.

INDEX

(Page numbers in *italics* refer to illustrations.)